How to Create Good Horse Training Plans:

The Art of Thin-Slicing

Hertha James

Powerword Publications,

133 Jackeytown Road

R.D.7 Palmerston North 4477

New Zealand

Muddy Horse Coaching

hertha.james@xtra.co.nz

www.safehorse.info

www.herthamuddyhorse.com

© Hertha L. James (2016)

Font: Bookman Old Style 11

Disclaimer of liability:

The author and publisher shall have neither liability nor responsibility to any person or entity with respect to any loss or damage caused or alleged to be caused directly or indirectly by the information contained in this book. While the book is as accurate as the author can make it, there may be errors or omissions.

Horses that show dangerous behaviors should not be paired with casual or inexperienced horse owners or handlers. Readers are entirely in charge of their own actions.

Risk Radar: When around horses, we must have our Risk Radar on at all times.

Cover Photo: by Hertha James, featuring Smoky during a session filming saddle pads and sheets blowing in the wind.

Photography by: Bryan James, Hertha James and Bridget Evans unless otherwise noted.

Some of the photos are taken from video footage, which decreases quality but allows illustration of an exact moment.

Dedication

This book is dedicated to all those people and horses who live in the backblocks far away from clinic venues and study buddies – the people who rely mainly on their own imagination and what they can glean from books and DVDs.

And to all the people who may be money-poor but rich with the enjoyment of being out and about with their horses.

Acknowledgements

This book is much improved due to the input from Colleen Spence and Bridget Evans.

Thank you, Glenys Daley, for a superb editing job.

And a special thank you to Larry Metcalf who's eagle eye picks out those commas and lost prepositions.

Any remaining errors are totally mine.

The Author   12

This Book Includes Free YouTube Links   13

Short Glossary   14

Chapter 1
Introduction   19

   My Viewpoint   20

Comfort Zones   24

   How We Care for our Horse   27

Why Write Training Plans?   29

Chapter 2

   How Will My Horse Know When He is Right?   35

   Revisiting the Basics of Reinforcement   42

     Free-Shaping Example   44

   What about Behaviors we don't want?   44

     1. Ignoring   45

     2. Examples of Incompatible Behaviors   45

     3. Inhibitors   47

Summary   49

Signals   50

A Bit of Cheer-Leading for Equine Clicker Training   54

Chapter 3

What Sort of Character is this Horse?   59

Four Character Types   61

   Group A: Horses Who Move their Feet Easily   61

    1. "Where's the party?"   61

    2. "I'm out of here!"   61

Group B: Horses who don't move their feet easily   62

    3. "Where's the grass?"   62

    4. "I'm worried about this!"   64

Category Characteristics   66

    1. Electric Yellow - "Yahoo, where's the party?"   66

    2. Red Alert – "I'm out of here!"   68

    3. Green - "Yeah, whatever, where's the grass?"   70

    4. Blue Mood – "I'm worried about this!"   71

Self-Assertion   73

Social Factor Continuum   75

The Chameleon Inside Our Horse   77

Sending Horses Away for Training   82

Chapter 4

What do we have in our Toolbox?   85

Venues   86

Time   88

Simulations   90

    Simulations without the horse   91

    Simulations with the horse   92

Objects and Obstacles   98

Body Extensions   104

    Halter and Lead Ropes   105

    Sticks & Swinging Ropes   108

Signal Awareness   113

    Sensitization and Desensitization   114

Large Signal Dilemma   115
The Language of Horses   117
Video Clips   119
Horse Folder   120
   Daily Diary Format   121
   Specific Task Diary   123
   Chart Format   124
      Clicker Training Logs   127

Chapter 5

Thinking about Pressure   137
   General Life Pressures Facing Horses   140
   Human Pressures   143
   High Level Awareness   147
   How We Add and Remove Pressure   152
      How we put pressure on our horse   152
      How we take pressure off our horse   153
   Pressure Expands Our Comfort Zones   154

Chapter 6

Planning: Setting Goals and Objectives   157
   The Nitty-Gritty of Planning   159
      Difference between Training Plans and IEPs   159
      Features of Useful Plans   160
      Visualizing a Whole Plan   164
   Thin-Slicing   164
      Successive Approximations   167
      General Key Points   169
   ABCD: Writing Behavioral Objectives   171

From Task to Behavioral Objectives   176
   Example of Slices Written as Behavioral Objectives   176
   Two-way Communication   180

Chapter 7

Writing Training Plans and IEPs   183

   The difference between Training Plans and IEPs   183
   How Horses do Thin-Slicing   183
   Thin-Slicing Revisited   185

Writing a Training Plan   188

   1. Deciding on the Training Topic   188
   2. Scoping the Topic   188
   3. Thin-Slicing the Overall Task into Behavioral Objectives   190
   4. The Basic Weave Task Defined   191
      Weave Illustrations   197
   Writing Individual Education Programs (IEPs)   203
   What an IEP does for the Horse   203
   What an IEP does for the Handler   204
      Patience Technique   206
   Hints for Writing Your IEPs   207

Chapter 8

A Training Plan for Ground-Tying   211

   The Prerequisites   213
      A. Standing Still – Teaching Parking   213
      B. Using Mats as Destinations   216
      C. Leading Willingly and a Nice Back Up   216
      D. Teaching the "Whoa" Voice Signal   216

    E. Rope Relaxation   217

  Ground-Tying Training Plan   218

    Generalization   228

    Short Summary of the Ground-Tying Training Plan   229

  Reminders   232

Chapter 9

Summary of the Planning Process   235

1. Decide on a Topic   235
2. Scope the Topic and Seek the Prerequisites   236
3. Define a Specific Task (ABCD)   237
4. Venues, Props and Time   239
5. Brainstorm Possible Thin-Slices   239
6. Slices in an Order that Might Work = Training Plan   239
7. Decide How You Will Document Your Progress   240
8. Experiment to Find a Starting Point   240
9. Outline your Individual Education Program   240
10. Tweak Your IEP   241

Conclusion   241

Appendix 1: Starting Clicker Training   243

  Materials: Gear Checklist   243

    Two Extra Points   246

  Method   247

    1. Simulation: Giving Meaning to the Click   247

    2. With the Horse   249

  Conclusion   256

Appendix 2:   259

Stages of Learning   259

Acquisition, Fluidity, Generalization and Maintenance   259
    Acquisition   259
    Fluency   260
    Generalization   261
    Maintenance   262

Appendix 3: List of YouTube Video Clips   264
    HorseGym with Boots Series   264
    Thin-Slicing Examples   267
    Free-Shaping Examples   268

Reference List   270

Other Books

The following books are also available from Amazon.com as hard copy or as e-books.

They contain lots of background material and numerous specific Training Plans.

- *How to Begin Equine Clicker Training: Improve Horse-Human Communication*

- *Conversations with Horses: An In-depth look at the Signals and Cues between Horses and their Handlers*

- *Walking with Horses: The Eight Leading Positions*

- *Learn Universal Horse Language: No Ropes*

If you prefer e-books but don't have a Kindle reader, Amazon has a free Kindle reader which can be downloaded to any computer, tablet or smartphone.

The Author

Hertha James grew up in Calgary just east of the Rocky Mountains. Her lifelong passion for horses began, age six, with a ride on a big black horse. Animals of all kinds have always been an important part of her work and leisure.

Hertha's career with animals began with a zoology degree and includes working as a zookeeper in Calgary and Wellington, New Zealand, as well as handling wild and exotic species for movie parts. Her animal experiences stood her in good stead when she changed careers to become a high school teacher of science and biology.

Hertha's other passion, writing teaching and learning resources, grew from her experiences as a teacher.

Teaching science to teenagers for 23 years honed her ability to structure information clearly. It taught her how to build new knowledge in small steps and integrate it with the information and beliefs already held by her students.

Hertha applies the same successful strategy to teaching horses and their handlers. She shows that horse training goals can be reached when valid starting points are based on gentle experimentation followed by good planning.

This Book Includes Free YouTube Links

Find my YouTube channel with a search for *Hertha MuddyHorse*. Please see Appendix 3 for a comprehensive list of titles. Relevant video clips are mentioned throughout the book.

These three playlists mainly relate to the ideas in this book.

1. *HorseGym with Boots*: these are numbered. For example, if you would like to view Clip #18, simply put "*#18 HorseGym with Boots*" into the YouTube search engine and it should take you there. Each title starts with its number.
2. *Free-Shaping*: These clips only have names. To find one, click on the playlist name and scroll down to find the title that you want.
3. *Thin-Slicing*: These clips also only have names so you have to scroll down the list to find the title you want to view.

Short Glossary

Behavior: that which is actually happening, not colored by our expectations or an emotional slant from our personal viewpoint.

Body Extensions: general name for the sticks, whips, wands, reeds, pointers, strings, ropes, halters, reins, bridles, saddles and harnesses that people use with horses.

Clicker Training: general name for training using the 'mark and reward' system. We can use a mechanical clicker, a tongue click, a special word or any special sound to *mark* the exact moment that the horse is doing what we want. The *marker sound* is immediately followed by a small food treat. See Appendix 1 for more information about clicker training.

Click&treat: the 'click' marks the exact behavior we would like. The 'treat' follows immediately after the click. The horse will seek to repeat the behavior that produced the click followed by the treat. Clicker training is also called the 'mark and reward' system.

Comfort Zone: a general term for all the places where we feel at ease. All the activities we can do without anxiety fall into our comfort zone. There is more about comfort zones in Chapter 1.

Criteria: the expectations that we set for a specific lesson. For example, if we are teaching side-stepping facing a fence line, the expectation (criterion) for our first lesson may be to get one sideways step, at which point we click&treat. If that goes well, we may shift the expectation (criterion) for our next lesson to two sideways steps before we click&treat.

Emotional Neutrality: the ability to stay calm and not buy into any upset that the horse or people around us are showing. Horses are highly tuned-in to the emotional state of other horses and people nearby. If we can remain calm, the horse is able to link in to our calmness. If we are nervous, afraid or fearful, the horse has no reason to feel comfortable with what we are asking him to do.

Free-shaping: using a *click&treat* to highlight any naturally occurring behavior we would like to 'capture' and make part of the horse's repertoire. For example, when we start clicker training by teaching the horse to touch his nose to a target object, we click&treat when the horse's natural curiosity causes him to touch his nose to our target.

We have 'captured' a behavior that was offered freely by the horse. We can then refine the behavior. We can ask the horse to move his head up, down, or to the side to touch the target.

We can ask him to move his feet to touch the target. Having the horse keen to seek out a target opens up a large range of training possibilities without the need for halters and ropes when we are in a safe, enclosed area.

Rather than putting pressure on the horse physically, we are setting him up with a puzzle and allowing him to solve it in his own time.

His motivation, rather than release of our signal pressure, is his instinctive seeking response to obtain more of what he likes (the treat that follows the click). There is more about this in Chapter 2.

Individual Education Program (IEP): anyone can write general Training Plans to teach something to a horse, but the horse's own handler has to refine a general Training Plan to best suit the character type, age, health and background experience of the individual horse to be educated.

Additionally, the IEP considers all the same factors in relation to the handler. For example, although I was athletic in my youth, aged knees now set a limit to how fast and far I can move.

Inhibitors: anything we do and use to keep ourselves, our horse and others around us safe. Inhibitors can be fences, ropes and reins that keep the horse contained in a safe area. Inhibiting actions include the use of our arms and body extensions to block behaviors that may harm the horse, the handler or others.

Mark & Reward Training System: see 'Clicker Training'.

Negative reinforcement: removing signal pressure (which might be very light) or discomfort. Stopping an action the horse understands as a signal, or stopping an action he finds bothersome.

Note, 'negative' is not used in the sense of being 'bad'. It is used in the mathematical sense of <u>subtracting</u> something (i.e. the signal pressure we have applied) from a situation. This is the most common type of reinforcement used by horse trainers.

Positive reinforcement: when the horse complies with a request, we highlight the moment with a marker signal and promptly deliver a treat. The treat has to be something the horse loves to receive, usually a tasty morsel.

Note that the term 'positive' is used in the mathematical sense of <u>adding</u> something to the situation, in this case a marker sound and a treat.

Many people think that the removal of their signal pressure is the 'reward' and therefore it is positive reinforcement. Actually, the release of the pressure is 'negative reinforcement' because the pressure has been removed.

This misunderstanding has led to a great deal of confusion for people trying to do their best with their horses.

Reflex action: a term used for an instinctive response. It is something we or any animal does without thinking about it first. A reflex action can be to move away, like jerking our hand away when it touches something hot. Maybe our whole body jumps away when we see a cockroach in our sock drawer.

Generally, reflex actions are concerned with physical safety. One good jolt from an electric fence can modify our behavior around electric fences for a long time.

Horses, being prey animals, rely on flight for safety and have a strong set of instinctive responses. We need to be aware of these and recognize them for what they are: the natural reflex actions of a prey animal.

Release reinforcement: this is simply another name for 'negative reinforcement' – releasing (removing) pressure.

Reward reinforcement: this is simply another name for 'positive reinforcement' – adding the click&treat reward.

Shaping: when we want to teach something, we experiment to see what the horse can offer already. Then we carefully develop an IEP which allows us, using very small steps, to influence the horse's behavior until he can confidently carry out the total task we want to accomplish.

Signal pressure: whenever we show up and want the horse to do things with us, we are exerting signal pressure. The pressure can become an extremely light message of communication once the horse understands what we want. In some circumstances, the pressure will be more intense if we have to clarify a message or if safety is our first concern.

Thin-slicing: cutting a whole task into its smallest teachable (clickable) parts so we can teach the horse in a way that keeps him being continually successful.

Threshold: the point at which we begin to feel uneasy about a situation. Our breathing rate and heart rate increase, we sweat and may get funny feelings in our gut. The same things happen to horses when they reach threshold. Their confidence turns to anxiety. The better we are at realizing when horses reach threshold, the more effective our training will be. This is because we can ensure that the horse stays near or at threshold while he is learning, but we don't tip him over threshold into fear reactions. Once a horse or a person is over threshold, constructive learning is no longer possible because anxiety emotions have taken over.

Training Plan: an outline of the possible thin-slices that we might be able to use to teach horses a particular task. A Training Plan is the starting point for writing a specific Individual Education Program (IEP) that suits a specific handler, the specific horse and the specific training environments that they have available. (See also, Individual Education Program.)

Chapter 1

Introduction

Teachers come in a couple of styles. One style points out your failings and prescribes ways to make you better. The other style suggests that you are just fine and offers suggestions you can take up to increase your knowledge and understanding.

I hope this book is written in the second style. And I hope that you will become a teacher in the second style for your horse.

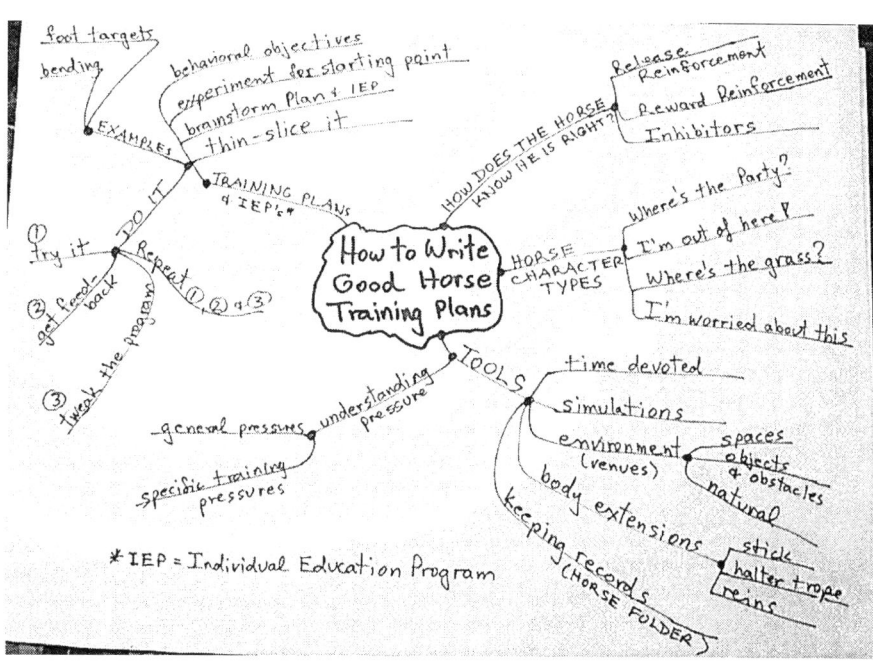

In many parts of the world, horses no longer bear the burden of commercial and military transport. Their burden has been shifted to provide:
- amusement and profit as in the racing industry
- business ventures such as Cavalia™
- business of breeding and/or training pleasure and competition horses

- channels for 'assertiveness training', 'team building' and 'leadership skills' for employees on a corporate 'day out'
- a medium for helping troubled children, teens and adults
- riding for the disabled (RDA™) organizations
- human recreation such as pony club, 4H, trekking, trail riding, driving and horse related competitive sports
- pet companionship.

My Viewpoint

Mark Twain said, *'It is just like man's vanity and impertinence to call an animal dumb because it is dumb to his dull perceptions'*.

For many people, it is not difficult to acquire a horse. But often horses are badly let down by well-meaning but uninformed owners. These horses are not offered the experiences and skills required to educate them for successful survival in the human centered world they live in.

Horses are frequent victims of benign neglect. They are left in paddocks or pens for days and weeks with little of interest happening and not much at all to stimulate their natural curiosity.

Horse training books and clinics often start with the viewpoint that horses have problems that need fixing. Sadly, this gives horse owners the idea that it is normal for horses to have 'problems' and that they have to somehow fix these problems.

In reality, no horse has a 'problem' until people force him to live an unnatural life and expect him to know things he has no way of knowing.

My view is based on the fact that people have removed horses from their natural horse existence. We hold them captive and expect them to do things that no horse living in the wild would ever consider doing, or need to do, in order to survive.

When we contain a horse, and use him for recreation, competition or a job, the horse is forced to contract with us. It seems to me, that in exchange for his body and soul, we need to put in effort to better understand what *being a horse* is like.

We can learn to be sensitive to how a horse sees, hears, smells, tastes things and feels with his whiskers. There is a section about this in my book, *Conversations with Horses: An in-depth look at the Signals & Cues between Horses and their Handlers*.

We need to understand how his circulatory and digestive systems work, so we can make his captive state as close to natural as possible.

Figure 1: Regular long-stem rough forage is a 'must' to keep a horse's gut bacteria in good shape. For 'easy keeper' horses on restricted calories, a hay net keeps the forage clean and gives the horse a small 'seeking' job to pull it out, although it doesn't solve the problem of regular whole-body movement to gain enough calories. Be wary of hay nets with holes big enough for your horse to put his foot through.

We should learn about the family and group dynamics of horses living naturally. We have to understand the importance and role of social order and self-assertion among horses.

People tend to see horses as a means to fulfil their own desires, much the same way as they view their bike or their car. They often have self-proclaimed 'professionals' train their horse and expect the horse to work by pushing certain buttons to get specific responses.

People often garage their flight animal in a stall as though it were a car. They want it handy for their needs. No thought is given to how confinement in small spaces affects a flight animal physiologically, mentally and emotionally.

Fortunately, more and more horse owners are taking a step back to look at the real nature of their horse. They are being creative with paddock configuration and how they feed their horses. They realise that 24/7 freedom of movement and access to low-energy forage are keystones to horse physical, emotional and mental health.

Figure 2: Rather than limiting horses to a square pen or small paddock, more horse owners are using creative electric fencing to both regulate grazing for 'easy keepers' and to set up more interesting environments for the horses.

More people are starting to realize that putting rugs on horses disturbs their finely tuned ability to adjust to temperature change. The owner may be feeling the cold, but the horse probably isn't.

More people are beginning to question the practice of nailing steel shoes to living tissue, which is a habit left over from Roman times when horses were first stabled and forced to stand in their own manure.

More people are becoming aware that putting a steel bar in a horse's mouth begins the process of salivation which in turn activates stomach acid to get ready to receive food. As no food is forthcoming, this is a good way to initiate stomach ulcers.

Putting a bit into a horse's mouth also breaks the natural seal of closed lips which allows horses to breathe with maximum efficiency. If you look at footage of horses running hard naturally, their mouths are tightly shut.

More people are beginning to look at their horse or pony as a companion animal with whom they can have a delightful relationship, whether they want to ride or not. People are learning to build a friendship bond with their horse, creating a relationship that resembles the friendship bond between natural horse herd members.

More adults are rediscovering the way of 'being together' that often arises naturally between children and their pets.

When we insinuate ourselves into a horse's life by taking the time to form a two-way relationship, the horse sees us as a member of his herd. He accepts us into his family grouping. He doesn't think he is part of our human social grouping.

This means that in a stressful situation, he will instinctively move in toward us, just as he would move into the center of a natural herd. The size difference puts us into a dangerous position.

While working as a zookeeper, I raised a caribou calf. Upon maturity, he looked upon me as a female caribou, which became a problem at rutting time, both for him and for me.

If a fearful situation activates the horse's flight response, he can hit the end of a rope or come to grief with fences - modern hazards for animals who have evolved in wide open spaces.

A horse is not simply a horse. Beyond breed characteristics, individual horses show different character types as well as different strengths and weaknesses. A horse coming into our care will have been profoundly affected by the relevant factors mentioned in this list:
- the nutrition and stress levels of his mother

- first experiences after birth
- all experiences since then
- nutrition as a foal, growing youngster and beyond
- ability to move and run freely (or not)
- relationships established with other horses (or lack of these)
- relationships established with people (good, bad, indifferent or none)
- type and nature of any training received
- foot care
- if ridden, the age when weight-carrying work was demanded of him and what he was asked to do, which will determine whether his joints developed without the added stress of being ridden young, jumped or asked to perform too many exercises such as circles
- whether the soft tissues of his mouth have been damaged from bits, plus the mental and physiological stresses associated with bits
- past injuries.

We may know all these things about a horse we have bred and raised ourselves. On the other hand, if the horse is purchased, we can't be certain about any of it.

The Training Plans and Individual Education Programs for a horse known from birth and handled daily will obviously start on a different page than the Training Plans and IEPs for a horse with an unknown or partially-known background.

This book outlines some of the tools we can use to set up carefully thin-sliced Individual Education Programs for each horse that comes into our life.

Comfort Zones

When we begin to do new things, it takes time and effort to get the feel of what we are doing. Getting this 'feel' for a new activity doesn't happen in ten minutes.

Doing something new takes us out of our comfort zone. We know when we are out of our comfort zone because our heart rate and breathing speed up. We may sweat more and have feelings of un-ease, often beginning in our gut or stomach.

It's important to recognise how we feel when we are out of our comfort zone, as well as how we feel when we are back in our comfort zone.

Only desire, effort and application can make our comfort zone larger. Learning and education are all about expanding comfort zones.

Obviously, both the handler and the horse have comfort zones. If both parties are out of their comfort zones, it may not be a good horse day. So, it's important that when the handler is out of his or her comfort zone, the horse is in his comfort zone.

When we take the horse out of his comfort zone, we ideally want to remain in our own comfort zone so we can maintain our emotional neutrality. By understanding our own and our horse's comfort zones, we'll have more good horse days until every day is a good horse day.

For a horse at a particular time, 'comfort' can mean the freedom to move and run, using up adrenalin and enlarging his personal space.

At another time the same horse may find 'comfort' in a quiet, restful state.

As the handler gets to understand the edges of a horse's comfort zone, it becomes easier and easier to thin-slice tasks to suit that particular horse.

The following diagram has six arrows that illustrate the six situations that a person or horse will come across.

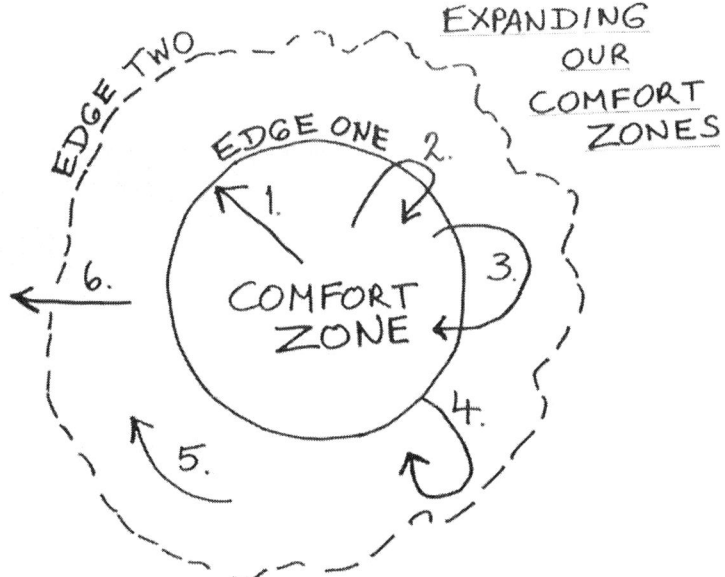

Figure 3: Comfort Zones: All of us, horse or human, have a 'comfort zone' within which our heart rate is normal and we can allow ourselves to relax. Expanding a comfort zone takes active intent. The six numbers are explained shortly.

The inner circle with the smooth boundary is the existing comfort zone. We can call this boundary 'Edge One' because it is a threshold that determines our behavior.

To expand our comfort zone, we must move out toward the broken line. Out there is the world with all kinds of thresholds. We can call the broken line 'Edge Two'.

The numbers with the arrows on the diagram refer to the six situations that will arise whenever a person or a horse is faced with expanding their comfort zone:
1. Lacking confidence to leave the comfort zone.
2. Can leave the comfort zone for a bit, but then must hurry back.
3. Able to leave the comfort zone for longer before going back.

4. No longer needs to retreat to the former comfort zone. The comfort zone has expanded.
5. Starting to feel comfortable well beyond the old 'Edge One' threshold.
6. I can do this now. What is the next challenge? I'm ready to set a new 'Edge Two'. 'Edge One' has moved out to encompass the original 'Edge Two'. The comfort zone has expanded.

If we push ourselves, or our horse, toward 'Edge Two' too quickly or too soon, we, or the horse, will feel worried, anxious or fearful.

We will 'run away' in our mind and make up reasons to avoid going 'out there' again. The horse will indicate that he'd like to leave the situation or he will 'shut down'. Either one means he has given up trying to understand what we'd like him to do.

This avoidance response is the brain's way of keeping us safe. It's a useful instinct in some situations, but in today's world, and with horses forced to live in captivity, we have to find ways of successfully expanding our comfort zones.

As we learn to recognize where we and the horse are in relation to our comfort zones for any given situation, we will be able to take more control of where we are, in relation to where we want to be.

Safety is always the priority. The horse has to learn how to respond appropriately to a variety of human pressures. The handler has to know how to move the horse to keep everyone safe when a stressful situation occurs.

A stressful situation can arise in a split second. It helps a great deal if the horse has faith in us and if we know how the horse will probably respond to a strong signal we may have to use when his adrenalin is up.

How We Care for our Horse

One option is to leave the horse in his paddock and vaguely look after him. The person may have become frightened by the horse and has lost motivation to spend time with him. If he needs to be moved, wormed or have his feet trimmed, he is tranquilized or traumatized by unaccustomed handling by people he doesn't know. I've seen this happen quite a lot.

Or perhaps the person's life is too busy to give a horse the time, care and devotion he needs to thrive in captivity. Occasional long rides and sporadic attention are not the cornerstones of a happy existence for a horse.

A domestic horse can thrive if someone makes the effort to spend regular time with him. It's also about teaching a horse correct responses to the pressures of captivity.

His life can be made better if he is taught, in a calm and thoughtful way, the basics such as:
- how to lead well on a loose rope
- move back on request
- navigate gates safely
- accept foot care
- worming and inoculations if these are necessary
- tie up
- travel safely.

My hope is that this book will make it easier for people to find a *starting point* to begin developing Training Plans and IEPs (Individual Education Programs). It's the old story about how does a Chihuahua eat an elephant? One bite at a time.

How does a dung beetle move an elephant dropping? By rolling away one tiny ball at a time. Or this wonderful saying, "Inch by inch, life's a cinch".

If a person has lost the confidence to be with their horse, there *is* a place to start rebuilding confidence. If a person has limited time to spend with their horse, there *is* a way to teach missing skills in tiny segments and sessions.

Vanessa Bee has written a book all about teaching key skills in a series of 3-minute sessions. You can find its details in the References section.

If there is a task the horse (or handler) is not yet able to do, the key word is <u>yet</u>. They can't do it <u>yet</u> because the time, thought and effort necessary have not yet gone into the teaching and learning process.

To teach or refine a behavior, we build on what's already there. We focus on what we can do, not on what we can't do yet.

Once we determine a starting point to teach a specific task, it's our job to find the flow of thin-slices that will take our teaching and the horse's learning from the starting point to the finished task we want to accomplish.

Why Write Training Plans?

The Training Plan is a generalized outline of the probable steps or thin-slices we might use to teach a horse a specific task.

The IEP is the Training Plan fine-tuned to take into account:
- the character type of the horse
- the personality of the handler
- their existing relationship
- what the horse can already do
- the skill sets of the handler
- the accessible training environments
- time available.

Figure 4: Finished Task: Boots has four feet firmly placed on a piece of plywood.

The task in Figure 4 looks simple, but a lot of thin-slicing went into building the confidence for Boots to step cleanly onto such a board at request in a variety of environments, and stay 'parked' on it until further notice. The thin-slices are outlined in a clip called *Thin-slicing the 1 Meter Board Task* in my *Thin-Slicing Examples* playlist.

As parents and teachers know only too well, influencing and changing the behavior of another person is neither easy nor straightforward. Students of any kind, human or horse, are not empty vessels into which we pour knowledge.

Every student - human, equine or canine - comes with personal knowledge, convictions and sensitivities which have to be factored into any teaching/learning situation.

Writing (and executing) good Training Plans, and the IEPs derived from them, is a pro-active way to help our horse become more confident and resilient. Whatever our reason for having a horse, we improve his life by teaching him appropriate responses to the pressures that humans impose.

We may want to:
- improve our riding
- improve our ground work
- ensure the horse loads and travels easily
- just have fun and enjoy our equine (horse, pony, donkey or mule) in a safe manner
- help our horse become a relaxed walking companion out and about the neighbourhood (walking or jogging with an equine has come to be called 'equicizing')
- keep a retired horse fit and interested in life
- teach a young horse how to respond safely to human pressures and build confidence with new spaces, objects and obstacles well before riding begins
- bring a rested or injured horse back into work slowly
- teach specific skills and manoeuvres for display, sport or competition

- keep our pet horse supple and moving to maintain his health
- play with Horse Agility (www.thehorseagilityclub.com).

Figure 5: Equicizing: We walk our dogs, why not our horses? Zoe and Boots pause for a drink during a walk on the farm tracks.

Figure 6: Horse Agility is great fun and gives a focus to horse time. Each month sees a unique arrangement of objects and obstacles to negotiate.

Every horse that enters our sphere of influence will have a different starting point for anything we want to teach. Each horse will be missing prerequisites that we need to fill in as part of his IEP derived from a general Training Plan.

The coming chapters look at these topics:
- how a horse knows when he is 'correct' in our eyes
- different horse character types
- tools that we can use and refine
- understanding pressure
- setting aims or goals; writing behavioral objectives
- examples of how to develop training plans and IEPs.

The approach in this book is one of 'constructing' or creating the behaviors we need and want our horse to offer. Each step of the way aims to encourage the horse and the handler to do what they *can* do, not what they *can't* do.

As the respective comfort zones of the horse and handler expand, the *'we can do that'* sphere gets larger and larger.

Teaching and learning are not the same thing. We may think we are teaching one thing but the horse may be learning something quite different from what we intended. If we are not careful, we can easily and unintentionally reinforce behaviors we don't want.

Most often this happens if the handler's timing is off so that signal pressure and intent are removed at the wrong moment, or the click is not timed to the specific movement or stillness that we want.

For example, if we are asking the horse to move his hind end away by touching him on the hip, the horse may at first move into the pressure rather than move away. If we remove our touch while the horse is moving into the pressure, we have just taught him that is what we want.

We have to retain our touch on his hip and our intent for him to move his hind end away, until he tries that as part of his experimentation to see what will remove our touch pressure.

The instant the horse shows an inclination to move away from our touch signal, we remove the pressure so the horse regains his sense of comfort. If we also click&treat, the horse has two assurances that he has done what we want.

Chapter 2 looks at how we let our horse knows when he's right.

Chapter 2

How Will My Horse Know When He is Right?

The behavior of any person or animal is shaped with three types of consequences. Let's look at them.

1. Something in the environment creates pressure. We respond to the pressure with *behavior that makes the pressure go away or get less*.
An example might be housework. When the floors need vacuuming, the toilet needs cleaning and the windows are hard to see through, pressure mounts up on me to stop doing more interesting things in order to get the cleaning done. At some point the pressure of the dirt causes me to behave in ways that result in a cleaner house.

Horses Too: When our horse is relaxed resting, grazing or socializing in his paddock, our arrival in his environment is a form of pressure. As soon as we put on a halter he has to give up what he was doing and respond to touch pressure via the rope. The horse is adjusting his life to read our intent and he changes his behavior to comply with our requests.

Figure 7: Boots 'in uniform' with her halter and lead rope.

When we are out for a walk in a grassy area, Boots would rather be seeking tasty bits of grass, but she recognizes her halter and lead as a 'uniform' which influences her behavior choices. If she cooperates with my signals, she can avoid pressure on her halter via the rope.

If we visit our horse with a pocket full of treats to play clicker training games at liberty, our presence with the treats is also pressure.

Behavior can also be shaped by creating a desire. If we feel dehydrated, we desire and value a drink of water, so we carry out the behaviors that enable us to get a drink.

2. It comes to the person or animal's attention that *behaving in a certain way earns a reward that is valued.*

If a person places a high value on organic food, he or she might carry out all the behaviors needed to plant and tend a vegetable garden in order to gain the reward of organic produce.

A person might sign up for a paid job which earns money that can be exchanged for needed or wanted items.

Horses too: If we decide to use equine clicker training, it comes to the horse's attention that if he behaves in a certain way, he can earn a 'click' marker signal immediately followed by an edible treat. Since horses (unless too upset or aroused) always enjoy a tasty morsel, food is the reward of choice for equine clicker trainers.

Figure 8: Boots is receiving her treat after jumping through the hoop behind her. When we use clicker training for jumping, we have to carefully chose the moment to click. Some horses try to go into treat-retrieval mode instantly, so it's safest to time the click to their landing.

There is a third way that behaviors can be shaped.

3. Something in the environment *inhibits* what the person or animal would like to do, so *their energy is re-routed into different behavior.*

It might be a perfect day to go fishing, but it's Tuesday and if we don't show up at work we will lose our job or a day's pay.

If you are a small child who likes to wander and explore, your parents might restrict your freedom of movement by putting up child proof fences and gates.

If you are a teen, your parents' expectations or your own desire to do well on an assessment might cause you to stay home and study rather than have an outing with friends.

Horses too: When we keep horses, we likewise inhibit their free movement. When we want the horse to 'study', we use fenced spaces, and/or halters and ropes to help keep the horse's attention on what we are doing.

In other words, we manage the environment to inhibit the horse's freedom to move when and where he wants.

Figure 9: When we take our horse into the wider world, we use inhibitors like lead ropes (or reins if we are riding) to keep everyone safe.

In most cases, we want to teach the horse behaviors that allow him to be safe in a human-dominated environment. We want to teach him to understand human pressures so he can become bolder and more resilient around people.

If a horse behaves in a way that is unsafe, such as pushing into us, we can use a gesture or a body extension to defend our personal space, just as another horse would use his neck, head, teeth, feet and tail to define his personal space when the need arises.

Defending our personal space is not the same as striking out toward the horse, which is an aggressive action. Horses easily understand the difference between aggression and defence.

If the horse attempts to push into us, we use actions that inhibit the pushing by directing the horse's energy into a different movement. If we then mark the alternative movement with a click&treat, we've used all three elements. We've changed the behavior we don't want and we have captured the behavior we do want.

To recap, here are the three elements that cause *changes in behavior*.

1. Something in the environment creates pressure. We respond to the pressure with a behavior that *makes the pressure go away* or get less.
2. It comes to the person or animal's attention that behaving in a certain way *earns a valued reward*.
3. Something in the environment inhibits what the person or animal would like to do, so their *energy is re-directed* into different behavior.

The first two elements *reinforce* a behavior. The third element stops or *inhibits* a behavior. Often all three of these elements work together to influence behavior.

Some equine clicker training enthusiasts strive to become purists and say they want to use only the second element (reward). They believe that showing the horse how to earn rewards can be used for almost all their training. However, if they use fences, ropes or reins, they are, by definition, using inhibitors.

More people use a healthy combination of all three elements. Every person and animal learns from the consequences of their actions. A desirable consequence can be release of pressure or it can be a reward. If we use clicker training, it is usually both.

How does the horse know he is right?

He knows he is right if he is reinforced for a specific behavior by the removal of pressure or if he gains a desirable reward. If we use rewards, the marker signal (click) which indicates that a reward is coming is usually simultaneous with the removal of the pressure.

When we use inhibitors, the horse knows he is right if he doesn't encounter an inhibitor. For example, if we've asked him to trot around us in a circle, we want him to keep trotting as long as we stay quietly neutral in the center. If he drops from trot to walk, we add energy that inhibits the horse's desire to walk. Using a bit of pressure as an inhibitor teaches him that trotting is right until we give a new signal.

We could also reward the horse with a click&treat for moving into a trot. At first, we would reward for the walk-trot transition, and teach a signal for the transition. Then we would click&treat for a stride or two at trot after the signal, then a few more strides, and so on. We gradually withhold the click to get duration of the gait.

Clicker-savvy horses know that the click means closure for the task they are doing. Horses become incredibly astute about waiting for the click. Done well, clicker training gives horses much appreciated clarity about what we'd like them to do.

If we are working the horse in a circle on a long rope or at liberty in a round pen, we can click&treat for a quarter circle, a half circle, a full circle, two circles, and so on, gradually extending the duration of the gait. The horse learns to keep walking, trotting or cantering until he hears the click that tells him to stop and retrieve his treat.

If we want the horse to walk around us in a circle and his desire is to trot, we lower the energy of the situation to inhibit the horse's desire to trot. In this way, we can show him that 'walk' is what we want until we give a new signal.

An alternative is to allow the horse to trot until he decides to walk, at which point we click&treat the walk. We can teach a trot-walk signal and reward with click&treat for the transition. Then we can gradually build up duration at the walk in the same way as described earlier for the trot.

At times, we begin teaching a specific signal by causing mild discomfort and releasing the discomfort the moment the horse responds in the way we want.

With experienced trainers, the 'discomfort' morphs into a very light signal which becomes information for the horse rather than actual discomfort.

The horse learns to seek the release. He tries various things until the release occurs. If the handler knows what he or she is doing *and is totally consistent* with the signal and the timing of the release, the horse quickly learns which response earns the release.

When we release signal pressure and click at the same time, then promptly deliver the treat, the horse gets two tiers of reinforcement that tell him he was right.

If we are free-shaping a behavior, the reward (click&treat) alone tells the horse that he was right and what he just did is what we want him to do. He will be motivated to repeat the behavior that resulted in the click&treat.

Whenever we change the context of the request, we have to carefully teach it again in the new context. The new context can be:

- a different gait (different energy level)
- a different environment
- a different handler
- different distractions.

Horses are very sensitive to the parameters within which they have learned something.

Boots and I play a game where she targets various parts of her body to my hand. She quickly builds an awareness of the order in which I ask her to do the targeting. If I change the order, I've changed a major parameter, and it takes a while for her to adjust to a new sequence of requests.

Here are examples of things Boots and I may do at the end of a session or as regular rainy day games. *#66 HorseGym with Boots* shows some of these in action.

1. Knee lifted to my hand.
2. Hind foot on same side lifted when I point to it (no hand connection).
3. Ear to my hand.
4. Chin to my hand.
5. Eye to my hand.
6. Head down with light touch on poll and up again with a knee gesture.
7. Shoulder to my hand.
8. Ribs to my hand.
9. Hindquarters to my hand.
10. Hindquarters moved away (no hand connection).

We do it once on each side of the horse, giving us twenty movements in total. If we do them in the order above, she is faultless. With practice, we can now successfully mix them up. The one she finds hardest to do in random order is number 2, the hind foot on same side lifted when I point to it. It's also one of the two tasks where she doesn't connect with my hand.

If we are mindful of how sensitive horses are to parameter changes, we'll try harder to remain consistent and allow extra learning time when we change parameters. It might seem like a tiny change to us, but horses are so aware that the change may be highly significant for them.

Often the human is unaware of the change he or she has made in body orientation or the placing of a touch signal or the nature of a gesture. But horses notice everything.

Revisiting the Basics of Reinforcement

We tell the horse when he is correct in our eyes by reinforcing the behaviors we want. As already mentioned, reinforcement has to be something the horse values.

Horses generally value a lack of pressure (comfort) and they value food.

A specific behavior is reinforced if *one or both* of the following happen.

1. The horse's behaviour results in *release* from pressure (greater comfort).
2. The horse's behaviour results in a *reward* that he values.

In terms of animal behavior literature, a *release* from pressure is called 'negative reinforcement' because the pressure has been REMOVED or SUBTRACTED from the equation. The term 'negative' is used in its mathematical sense, not in its everyday meaning of 'bad' as compared to 'good'.

If we add something desirable to the equation, animal behavior literature calls it 'positive reinforcement' because we have ADDED something to the equation. Again, the word 'positive' is used in its mathematical sense, not in its everyday meaning of 'good' as compared to 'bad'.

Whenever we reinforce a behavior with a *release* of pressure, with a *reward*, or with both, we increase the likelihood that our horse (child, dog, wife or husband) will repeat that behavior.

It is common for people to mistakenly think that releasing the pressure of their signal is a reward. Hence there is a great deal of confusion about the difference between release (negative) reinforcement and reward (positive) reinforcement.

In terms of training or teaching, a reward is something desirable *added* to the situation, not the removal of pressure applied.

Once we understand this distinction, we can see how reward reinforcement by itself can 'free-shape' a horse's behavior without the need for halters and ropes.

Free-Shaping Example

For readers not yet using equine clicker training, an abbreviated *Getting Started with Clicker Training* is available in Appendix 1 at the back of this book.

Before delving into clicker training, be sure to use the information in Appendix 1 to work out the fundamentals of safe food delivery with the horse.

For more detailed information, please see my book, *How to Begin Equine Clicker Training: Improve Horse-Human Communication.*

If we want our clicker-savvy horse to walk along with us without needing a halter and rope, we can free-shape this behavior by using his natural curiosity. If we appear in his paddock with a pocket full of carrot strips, he may come over and earn a click&treat for coming over.

If we move alongside his neck and take a step forward, he may well take a step with us and earn a click&treat. We might then take two steps and if the horse walks with us he earns another click&treat. And so on, gradually increasing the number of steps to as many as we like.

If you use the *one click = one treat* dynamic, clicker-savvy horses will halt when they hear the click.

If the horse gives up coming along with you, you have added more steps too fast or his attention has shifted to something else. If the horse reaches a plateau, go back to fewer steps and shorter training sessions. Once the horse understands the game, vary the number of steps you take before the click&treat.

#83 HorseGym with Boots demonstrates the process. An older clip called *Ex. 7 Shadow Me at Liberty* in my *Thin-Slicing Examples* playlist also shows this in action.

What about Behaviors we don't want?

If we want to *reduce the likelihood* of a particular behavior, we have three choices.

1. Ignore it
2. Teach a behavior we do want that is incompatible with the one we don't want.
3. Apply inhibitors.

1. Ignoring

When a human baby is born, we stop puddles and worse by using an inhibitor in the form of a diaper (nappy). At some point, we encourage the child's ability to recognize the need to delay urinating in time to reach the potty.

At first there will be accidents because the child is still learning that he or she can control the relevant sphincter muscle.

So, what shall we do when there is a puddle on the floor? Our safest bet is probably to downplay its importance (since we can't totally ignore it as it needs cleaning up), treat it as relatively unimportant and wait until the potty *is used* to give maximum parental attention and a reward.

Basically, when our student can't yet achieve our aim, we quietly reset the task and watch closely for something to reward and celebrate.

Horses too: when the horse is in the process of learning something new, and can't yet achieve it, it's best to simply relax after the attempt, quietly reset the task and try again.

At the same time, we keep on splitting the overall task into units (slices) so small that it becomes hard for the horse to *not* achieve what we are asking.

We will look at the detail of thin-slicing in later chapters.

2. Examples of Incompatible Behaviors

If a horse has a tendency to nip or bite, we teach him to back up. Not only does that give him something to do, it also puts us out of reach of his mouth when we are not purposefully delivering his treat.

With reward reinforcement (via clicker training), the horse quickly learns that a click&treat is only forthcoming if he steps back on request or at least keeps his nose turned away.

We can teach the horse to back up a step or two while he is still behind a safe fence or gate. The barrier has to be low enough to let us reach across it easily. We step toward the horse and hold the treat toward his chest so that he has to step back to retrieve it from our hand. Then we can ask him to step forward again to touch a target we are using, earning another click&treat. (Details about this in Appendix 1.)

Once the horse understands to step back we add, signals (touch, gesture, voice, energy, intent) to the movement. Now we have a way of asking the horse to back up and step forward in any situation.

With many short repeated sessions, a new behavior becomes a habit. Used often and consistently, it becomes a strong habit. We have taught a desirable behavior incompatible with the behavior we don't want (biting, nipping, mugging). If we are consistent, the old nipping habit is replaced by the new behavior of backing up a step or two.

We can use the positioning of our treat hand to help teach a variety of moves. One example is using 'food hand' placement to turn the forehand away (click&treat) before asking the horse to walk on in a new direction. This is useful for a horse that tends to push his shoulder into the handler.

If a horse easily becomes anxious and high-headed, we can use reward reinforcement to teach him a signal to lower his head, which triggers relaxation hormones.

A short video clip called _Single Challenge: Free-Shaping Head Lowering_, found in my *Thin-Slicing Examples* playlist, shows this in action. The second clip on the same topic shows the importance of putting a new task 'on signal'.

Once horses have a strong history of reward reinforcement for dropping the head at times of anxiety, they have been known to 'self-medicate' even if the handler is not there to click&treat their action.

If a horse working on a circle tends to 'fall in' so his circle becomes smaller and smaller, we can use release and reward reinforcement together to teach a 'move out please' signal. Gesture pressure toward the shoulder asks the horse to widen the circle. When he does, a click&treat tells him that he interpreted our gesture correctly.

3. Inhibitors

It's hard to talk about positive and negative inhibitors in the same way that we talk about positive (reward) and negative (release) reinforcers.

If we have our horse in a fenced area, are we ADDING the fence to the equation or are we SUBTRACTING the horse's ability to move further away?

If my horse wants to eat grass when I am wanting to exercise her at a trot on the lunge in a grassy paddock, I can inhibit her grass-diving behavior by giving it an undesirable consequence such as a tag on her butt with the end of my lunging whip or stick and string combination.

It puts her in the position of having to choose between the attraction of the grass and the unwillingness to have her butt tagged. I'm using the tag game to inhibit her desire to dive for grass in that particular context.

Animal behavior literature talks about positive and negative punishment, again using the terms in the mathematical sense.

Positive punishment means adding an undesirable consequence (hitting, whipping, spurring, jerking and putting pressure on the halter or reins).

Negative punishment means removing something desirable or comfortable (food, water, friends, freedom to move, freedom to open the mouth by using a cross-over noseband).

But the word 'punishment' in the English language comes with a great deal of baggage. I don't think it is a useful word in terms of teaching our children, our horses or any other animal.

If our horses or dogs are behind a fence, tied up, on a lead, or if a horse is being ridden, it would seem that they are in a perpetual state of 'negative punishment' because we have *taken away* their freedom to move and do what they want.

Or are they in a perpetual state of 'positive punishment' because we've added the lead or reins or fences to inhibit their free movement?

I think the term 'inhibit' is more suitable. Roger Abrantes, a European animal behaviorist, when translating his work into English, found that the word 'punish' had too many emotive meanings for people. He thinks that the English word 'inhibit' better expresses what we do when we train animals. We have to inhibit certain behaviors in order to keep ourselves, the horse, and others around us safe at all times.

Horses in paddocks or fields are obviously inhibited from roaming anywhere by fences. But they can move freely at any pace, be aware of what is going on in their field of view and enjoy good weather.

Figure 10: We have to inhibit our horses from roaming free, but we can maintain their ability to move at any pace, seek food naturally and enjoy a lovely day.

Horses in small yards would be similar to people on 'home detention'. They are restricted to a small space but can at least stand in the sun, walk around a little bit, see what's going on in their neighborhood but not join in.

Horses in stalls are in isolation units. They can't walk out, enjoy a nice day or see much of anything. They can only shuffle in a small circle.

At some point, containing a horse changes from inhibiting him from dangers in the wider world to the cruelty of punishment. Punishment is when we take away his ability to engage in free movement, natural grazing, enjoy the sun, entertain his curiosity and interact with his friends.

We all have our desires inhibited to some extent. It is a matter of degree.

A horse living in the wild has his behaviors inhibited or influenced by higher ranking horses, by the need to find adequate food and water, and by his need to be aware of predators and other dangers.

It's easy to forget that wild horses live in environments where food shortages during summer drought and winter snowfall dominate life and actions. During summer, adequate water supply can also be a huge limiting factor. The enchanted view that many people have of the life of wild horses is more fantasy than fact.

Summary

Let's get back to the question.

How will my horse know when he is doing the 'right' thing?

1. When I remove or decrease *signal pressure* at the moment of a 'correct' response ('correct' from the handler's point of view, of course), so increasing the horse's state of comfort.
2. When I mark the desired behavior with a special sound followed by a desirable treat. The marker sound is

usually simultaneous with the removal of the signal pressure, so the 'mark & reward' system (clicker training) has two ways of letting the horse know he is right. Most horses learn quickly and enthusiastically with carefully applied clicker training. See Appendix 1 for details about getting started with clicker training.
3. When I remove or decrease any *inhibiting pressure* being applied with body language, ropes, reins or body extensions, so increasing the horse's state of comfort.

Signals

Chapter 5 looks in more detail about understanding pressure, so the emphasis here is on the types of signals we use to communicate with a horse.

Whenever we are with our horse and ask him to do something, we are applying signal pressure. The pressure may be so light it is invisible to a casual observer.

Careful training turns signal pressure into a secret language between the horse and the handler. At times the pressure can become stronger if something has upset the horse and we need to keep everyone safe.

Figure 11: Bridget is using body language to signal Boots to turn right. She might also blow gently into the horse's ear!

A comprehensive look at the topic of signals is found in my book, *Conversations with Horses: An In-Depth Look at the Signals & Cues between Horses and their Handlers.*

Very Brief Overview about Signals

A signal can be body language, body orientation, a word, a gesture, touch, energy level, intent, or a certain place where we usually do a particular thing.

A signal can also be something in the environment we have made significant to the horse, like a mat, tarp, nose target or a log we jump often.

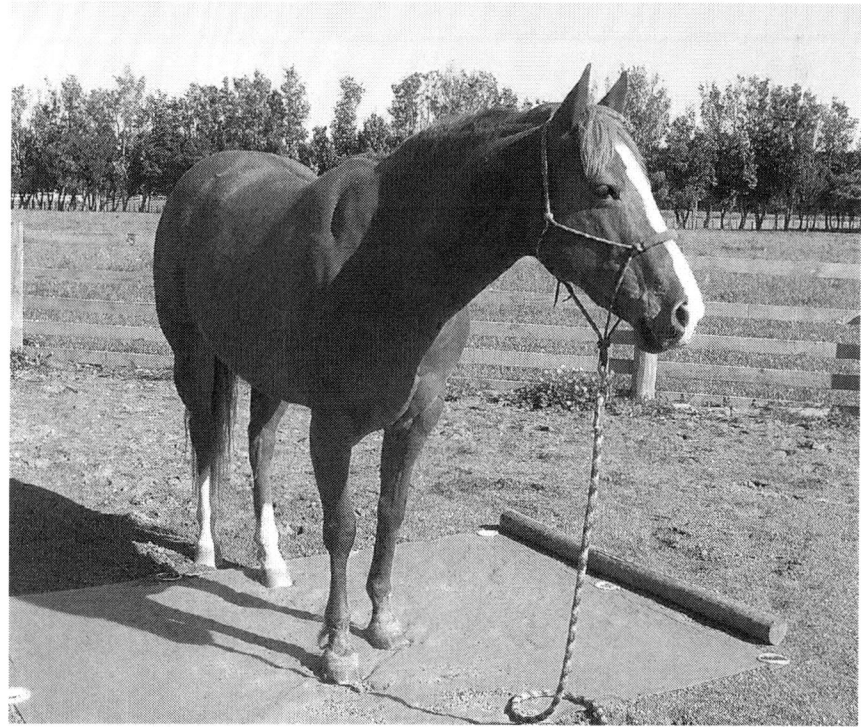

Figure 12: Due to a strong history of reward reinforcement relating to a tarp, the tarp itself has become a signal for Boots to come and stand on it. When I appear with a tarp she loves to approach and 'help' set it out as soon as she sees it.

Often our signal consists of several signal elements used at the same time. We can call these signal bundles or multi-signals.

What defines a signal is that the meaning of the message sent is the same as the meaning of the message received.

Good horse trainers can quickly build a language the horse understands because good horse trainers understand the many signals that the horse is giving as they respond or react.

Your aim might be to take your halter and lead into the paddock to fetch your horse. The horse may see this as a signal that you are going to do fun things together. He may come over as soon as he sees you with the halter. You and the horse are in agreement about what the halter means. It is a useful signal in your relationship.

If the horse sees you with the halter and moves away, he is clearly reading your intent, but he is not in agreement with your plan. So the halter in your hand is not a signal useful to your relationship because what you want it to mean (we are going to spend time together) does not raise the same desire in the horse.

The starting point for an Individual Education Program for this horse would deal with changing halter-avoidance behavior into halter-loving bchavior.

The first horse I bought in New Zealand was an ex Pony Club gelding about 16 years old. I was able to take over the rent of the paddock he shared with a group of other horses, so I did not have to move him after the purchase.

The first time I went to see him, it took me four hours to 'catch' him. I walked behind him with a bucket of food for four hours until he decided, "She's not going to leave me alone so I may as well check out the bucket".

When I initially went to see him, he was already 'caught' and haltered. I have no idea whether he was in a happy relationship with his former owner or if she and her father had spent several hours catching him. It's a good idea to always show up early when going to look at a horse you may want to buy.

The next time it took about two hours to catch him. I can't remember what happened after that. We must have eventually come to an agreement because we had a long, enjoyable relationship and did lots of things together. He remained wary of strangers and I never worried about anyone stealing him or cutting off his tail.

We can't expect a horse to understand what we want him to do unless we have taken him through a careful teaching program to explain what our signals mean, and for him to agree about what they mean.

Any signal we give our horse has *timing, intensity* and *duration*. If the signal is poorly timed, the horse may not notice it or be busy doing something else. Picking the right opportunity, and timing the signal well, are both important.

The *intensity* of a signal will vary with:

- what we are asking
- the level of education the horse has about that signal
- how carefully we have remembered to make the signal as light as possible
- the context of the situation; if danger is involved, our signal may have to become more intense until a situation is defused.

Signal *duration* will depend on what we are doing. We may use a *'constant on'* signal as when we ask for the horse to back up. Or we may use an *'on-off'* signal as when we ask the horse to walk on, turn, halt, trot or canter.

When we are riding or moving with the horse on the ground, our body movement flowing with the horse's movement gives the horse further information about what gait to maintain after the initial signal is turned 'off'.

Figure 13: Once I've asked Boots to 'walk on' around this obstacle, the movement and orientation of my body will draw her along without the need for any other signals.

If we nag with what should be an 'on-off' signal, such as bumping continuously with our legs when riding, or keeping the rope tight when we are leading, the horse gets no release and the action stops being a meaningful signal for a specific behavior change.

A Bit of Cheer-Leading for Equine Clicker Training

Clicker training is covered in detail in my book:
How to Get Started with Equine Clicker Training: Improve Horse-Human Communication.

If you have access to YouTube, you can get an idea of how to get started and how to progress to more complex training by viewing the series of clips found in my *HorseGym with Boots* playlist. You can find the first clip by putting *#1 HorseGym with Boots* into the YouTube search engine.

The book, of course, has much more detail and includes eight training plans that can be used as springboards for writing Individual Education Programs (IEPs) that suit you and a specific horse.

I adopted clicker training as part of my training kitbag quite a few years ago. Now I can't imagine being without it. Clicker training does require learning a few new skills and improving consistency. Since consistency is the foundation of any training, it is a good skill to improve.

If you are not yet an equine clicker trainer but would like to experiment with it, Appendix 1 outlines a starting process. Experimentation may lead you to incorporate it into your horsemanship toolbox.

Clicker training is not something that can be done ad-hoc when we feel like it, but it is easily integrated with the simple release reinforcement that everyone uses already.

Most equine clicker trainers use a tongue click or special sound/word rather than a mechanical clicker requiring hand action. With horses, we often need both our hands for other things.

Once we are in the habit of carrying treats in our pockets or a pouch, and have taught the horse polite table manners, click&treat easily becomes an integral part of our training.

All animal actions are geared toward *identity* (with group or place), *security* (of food and shelter) and *stimulation*. Horses living in the wild lead a life full of all sorts of stimulation and challenges.

It's hard for us to provide the same level of stimulation for our captive horses. The lucky ones spend their non-human time with other horses, moving freely 24/7 in large fields or on a track system.

Teaching our horse useful and fun things with click&treat reward reinforcement is one way to add stimulation to a life that may otherwise be exceedingly boring.

Figure 14: Using clicker training to have fun with a horse enriches both the horse's life and our life.

When we use clicker training correctly, it becomes so much easier to let the horse know the precise moment he is 'correct'. We click at the moment of the action (or relaxation) that we want.

The click buys us time to reach into our pocket or pouch and produce the treat. The treat is delivered in a firm, flat hand on an outstretched arm.

If there is no click, there is no treat. Once the horse has learned a few basic movements such as targeting our outstretched fist or backing up, it's easy to ask him to do something we can click&treat, even if we are just visiting to check up on him.

Until the horse has learned reliable food-retrieval habits, it's important to keep a safe fence or gate between the horse and the handler. Some horses get very excited when food is first introduced into the training regime. The horse must not be hungry when we use clicker training. A hungry horse may easily get too excited or too aroused to learn well. If the horse has a full stomach and still finds it super exciting, it can help to use lower value treats. If the horse is tentative, we can use higher value treats.

High value treats for Boots are bread, apple slices, feijoas and tomatoes, with peppermints as a top favorite. Lower value treats are pony pellets, celery and popped popcorn. Carrot slices sit somewhere in the middle. But she loves her food, so works happily for most sorts of treats. Some horses are more limited in their tastes.

My friend's horse, Smoky, who features on the cover, is extremely dubious about any new foods. He pulls faces when tasting something unusual and likes to stick with carrots and pony pellets, although he began to enjoy tomatoes when he saw how much Boots liked them.

By experimenting with a variety of items, your horse will let you know which he considers low value and which he considers high value.

If we are teaching with release reinforcement by itself, spot-on timing of the release is crucial if we want the horse to be able to understand exactly what we want.

It's hard for a casual horse owner to develop the 'horse-reading' and 'release-of-pressure' skills demonstrated by top-level horsemen and women.

For the casual horse owner, it's much easier to work with a plan that looks for the best moment to mark with a click, followed by a treat.

Rather than worrying about taking the pressure off the horse when we should, we can enjoy looking for the moments we can click because the horse is doing exactly what we want. If the horse is in the early stages of learning something new, we click the closest approximation to what we eventually want.

When we compare release and reward reinforcement, we are actually contemplating two very different ways of looking at the world, at our horse, and how we do things.

The two viewpoints have a strong similarity with two different child-raising or teaching philosophies.

One style focuses on pointing out faults and keeping pressure on until the child complies. The other style tends to ignore faults and provide reward whenever the child is doing the desired thing (or not doing the undesirable thing).

One parent or teacher wants to mold the child based on some sort of mental image. The other parent or teacher allows the child to unfold naturally with guidance and assistance (and discipline at times) to fit into society smoothly.

Horses too: Horses are often molded into competitive routines. Their training and experiences with people may be limited to a small skill set.

Other horses have a more diverse life, and the sort of training that makes them more resilient in a variety of situations. A few years ago, a New Zealand thoroughbred named Kiwi won the prestigious Melbourne Cup. When he wasn't racing, Kiwi plied the hills of his owner's sheep farm doing stock work.

Horses build strong bonds with other horses and with empathetic humans in their lives. When we take the time and trouble to build a clear, trusting two-way communication system with our horse using reward reinforcement, we can have great fun teaching our horse new things and learning along with him.

Have a look at Appendix 1.

We can put a halter on a horse by cornering him and forcing it on. I know horses whose halters never come off. Or we can teach the horse, in progressive steps and with reward reinforcement, how to put his head into a halter that we hold open for him. For more about this, including a video clip link, see the Training Plan in Chapter 4 - *Clicker Training Logs*: Example One.

I hope this chapter has given you information to help create a clear vision of how you will let your horse know when he is right.

The next chapter looks at different horse character types. If we understand and appreciate different character types, it will be much easier to write an Individual Education Program (IEP) to suit a particular horse.

Chapter 3

What Sort of Character is this Horse?

As soon as we have interaction with more than one horse, it is clear that horses come with different character types. This is not surprising, as the same is true for people, dogs and every type of animal we have as a pet or that zookeepers and researchers work with.

To teach effectively we have to know the nature of our audience. Good teachers and speakers are effective because they put time and energy into understanding their audience.

During my teaching career, I often had three classes of different abilities at one level in the curriculum. Three separate plans were necessary. The children who struggled needed more thin-slicing and reached a different point from the other groups when the time for a topic was up.

The academic children needed fewer basics, so the topic went at a faster pace and there was time to explore interesting tangents. The third group was somewhere in the middle.

When our 'audience' is the horse we want to teach, it pays to look closely at his character type and become aware of what sorts of things he finds hard, what motivates him, and what he enjoys doing.

A horse who is exuberant and light on his feet is great fun for a handler who can bring out and harness these attributes. Such horses tend to be confident and self-assertive.

Another type of horse may feel the need to flee at the smallest hint of possible danger. He does best with a training program that recognizes his anxiety. We can increase the confidence of such horses by carefully teaching layers of comfort and tolerance. The fear-flight response of this type of horse is always close to the surface.

A horse whose main aim in life is to seek out the next blade of grass presents a totally different challenge if we want to make our idea his idea. Such horses are usually energy-conservers and tend to be confident and bold in their home environments.

A horse who tends to 'freeze' when confronted with some of the bewildering things that people do is keeping his anxiety inside. He may appear 'quiet' to a casual observer, but he has shut himself down and is trying to hide in his personal mental 'happy place'.

This behavior may be related to the 'shutting down' that occurs when a prey animal knows it is about to be killed and eaten. Horses who tend to 'shut down' are innately shy and easily made anxious when things are happening too fast for them in their training regime.

It's possible to analyse more closely and come up with a large number of categories and sub-categories of horse character types.

Some authors have done this, using a variety of different criteria. Reading their work, I find that my eyes and mind start to glaze over after about the fourth category.

So we'll stick with four groups. That's enough to give us a good start with understanding horse character types and modifying our training to suit each one.

When we write a general Training Plan to teach a specific behavior or task, our focus is mainly on how we can thin-slice the task into its smallest teachable bits.

However, when we write an Individual Education Plan (IEP) for a particular horse, we recognize and incorporate the underlying features of his character type. Then we can adjust the program to cater to the way the particular horse learns most easily and responds most positively.

In this way, a general Training Plan becomes a specific program for a specific horse working with a specific handler in a specific environment.

Four Character Types

We can begin by distinguishing two general types of horses in terms of how easily they move their feet. Then we can divide each of these into two further groups, giving us four character types to consider.

Group A: Horses Who Move their Feet Easily

A horse might move his feet easily for one of two reasons.
1. He is innately an exuberant horse.
2. He has a high-level fear response.

1. "Where's the party?"

Exuberant & Confident: this category includes horses that seem to enjoy movement for its own sake.

Figure 15: This is Sonny with Amy, showing enthusiasm and exuberance. Photo by Carlin Connelly

2. "I'm out of here!"

Anxious & High Flight Response: this category includes horses whose first instinct, when they don't understand something, is to move away quickly.

Figure 16: This is Fareed learning about flags with Amy. His body language tells us that he is poised for flight. His faith in Amy and her careful training give him the courage to stay.
Photo by Carlin Connelly

Group B: Horses who don't move their feet easily

A horse may be reluctant to move for one of two reasons.

3. He's perfectly happy being a paddock potato.
4. He is too worried about the consequences of moving.

Reluctance to move can of course also be due to pain or soreness, so we need to check these out first.

3. "Where's the grass?"

Confident & Energy-Conserving: this category includes horses who have a chilled out view of life. They often easily put on weight. In the wild, they have the best chance of surviving food shortages during severe winters and dry summers.

My horse, Boots, is this type. Her approach to life includes a cost-benefit analysis of each situation before she uses up energy. Some people find this type of horse quite frustrating.

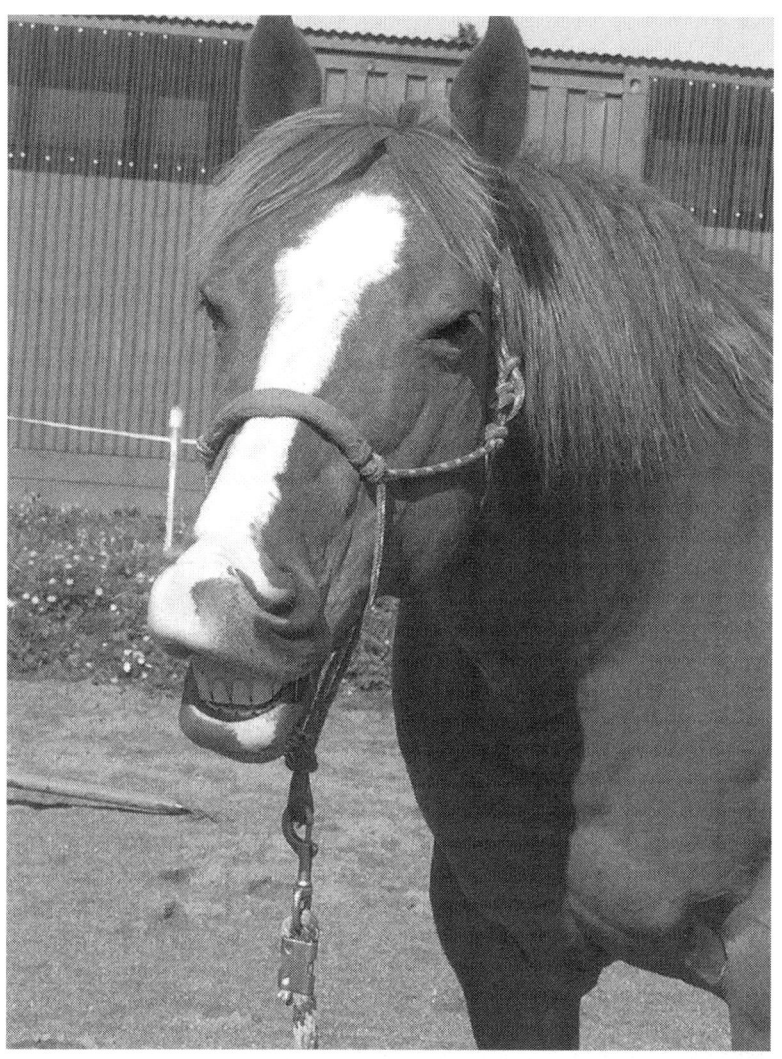

Figure 17: Boots is a laid back horse whose main concern is usually her next bit of grass. Her favorite activities are ones she can do standing still, like her 'smile'.

The <u>*January 2016 clip*</u> of Boots doing a Horse Agility course can be found in my playlist called *2016 OLHA*. (OLHA stands for 'Online Horse Agility'.) If you are able to watch it, note that Boots finds the 'wait' easy. However, shifting up into a trot, when I'm not trotting as well so she can match her energy to mine, is much harder for her.

4. "I'm worried about this!"

Anxious & 'stuck': this category includes horses who tend to become rooted to the spot if they don't understand something. They appear quiet to a casual observer. Their tension is held inside. If pressure gets too great, they can explode out of their stillness, creating a danger to themselves or anyone nearby.

Some enter a cataleptic state with head low and mind tuned out completely.

Figure 18: This is Scotty the first time he met the big ball. You can see from his stance, high head and worried expression that he is 'stuck'. He is an innately anxious horse who takes his confidence from Fiona, his owner.

When I first went to see a 14-year-old Thoroughbred mare that I eventually bought, she was tied up, standing very quietly. At the time, I just thought her stance was a bit spread-eagled and her head held rather low.

Now, ten years smarter, I know that she was holding her anxiety inside. It took about two years to gain her full confidence. When I first got her she did not know how to experiment when she was presented with a new challenge; she just 'froze'.

Summary of the Four Horse Character Types

1. "Where's the Party?" (bold, exuberant).
2. "I'm Out of Here!" (high-level flight response).
3. "Where's the Grass?" (energy-conserving paddock potato).
4. "I'm Worried about This!" ('stuck'- easily anxious about a new situation).

We'll shortly look at some of the words that people often use to describe each of these types of horses. But it is important to remember that the categories are a fluid continuum, not pigeonholes.

An individual horse may show only some of the characteristics in a list. Additionally, an individual horse can show the category characteristics strongly, moderately or only mildly.

Observing a horse at home in his usual environment, around horses and people he knows, gives us the clearest picture of his innate character type.

The staunchest energy-conserving paddock-potato horse at home may well turn into an *'I'm out of here'* horse taken somewhere new. Or he could turn into an *'I'm quietly worried about this'* horse.

A *'quietly worried about this'* type of horse, with careful teaching and lots of time to make up his own mind about things, might become a secret party animal in the right circumstances.

Although a horse may fit nicely into one of the categories described below most of the time, the categories run into each other and are fluid, depending on the environment in which the horse finds himself.

You may find it fun to color code the categories. The colors give us a shorthand way of thinking about the reactions of a horse when we are engaged with him. It can help us to recognize when our horse switches categories.

1. Electric *Yellow* — "Yahoo, where's the party?"
2. *Red* Alert — "I'm outta here."
3. *Green* — "Yeah, whatever, where's the grass?"
4. *Blue* Mood — "I'm quietly worried about this."

Just to repeat: a horse may innately fit nicely into one of these categories, but circumstance and environment can cause him to behave differently.

Category Characteristics

1. Electric Yellow - "Yahoo, where's the party?"

a) <u>Things to look for</u>: Most horses will show a few of these characteristics clearly, but not necessarily all of them. Any characteristic can show up as mild, moderate or strong.

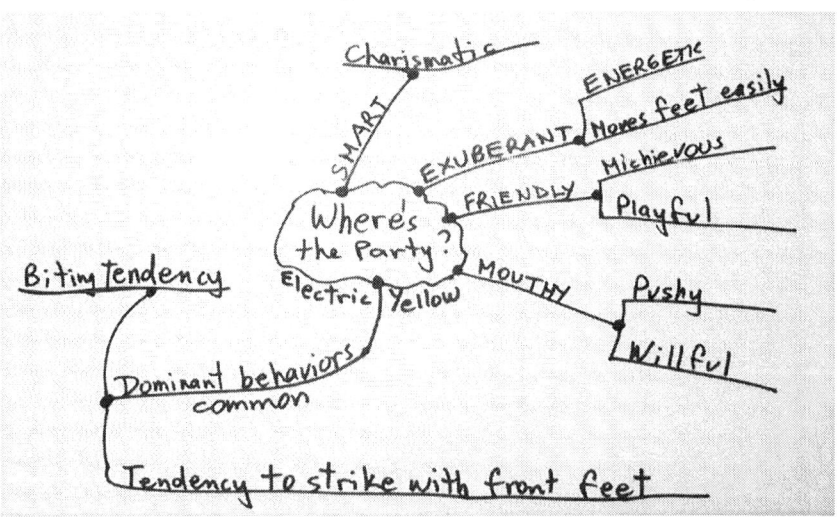

Figure 19: Characteristics of confident, exuberant horses who love to move.

b) <u>Once you have gained his confidence</u>, this type of horse is usually curious, smart, playful, and willing.

Useful Training Concepts

- Teach and encourage creative movement.
- Play with tasks using a variety of objects and obstacles.
- Plan new things to learn – provide as much variety as you can.
- See how many different things you can do with individual obstacles or objects.
- Be consistent with signals but teach a variety of tasks.
- Plan new environments to explore when he is ready.
- Create training plans and IEPs that keep up with his ability and energy.
- Reward-based reinforcement in the form of equine clicker training makes it easier to keep the horse's focus on what we want.

c) *What horses like this might find hard*:

- obedience - they get distracted by wanting to *have fun* in their own way
- yielding the forequarters - due to their strongly self-assertive nature
- backing up - this is best taught as a game rather than with pressure
- use of touch energy - usually respond well to light gesture signals which may work better than actual touch during ground work
- all parts of circles - due to circles being boring; creative circling is best
- aggressive people - will tend to make them respond aggressively
- wimpy people - will not be seen as worthy of attention
- boring work - will motivate them to make their own fun.

2. Red Alert – "I'm out of here!"

a) *Things to look for:* Most horses will show a few of these characteristics clearly, but not necessarily all of them. Any characteristic can show up as mild, moderate or strong.

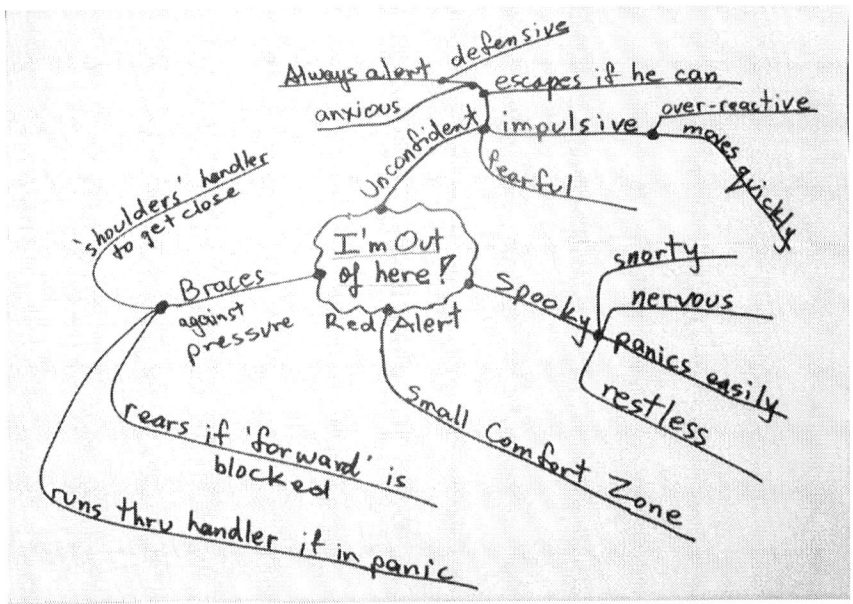

Figure 20: Characteristics of flighty-type horses who feel the need to move their feet when they feel anxious because they don't understand what is wanted.

b) *Once you have gained his confidence* and become his 'safe harbor', this type of horse can be athletic, perceptive and sensitive.

Useful Training Concepts

- Safety is always this horse's first concern.
- Recognize thresholds and use lots of retreat, which gives him opportunities to make up his own mind about the safety of what you are asking him to do.
- Whenever necessary, allow him to pause and access a safe place where he can regain calmness.

- Allow him to burn off adrenalin when he goes into reactive flight mode, but also look to interrupt patterns that are of no benefit by directing him into an easy task he already knows and is able to do.
- Have a strong focus on what you want.
- Be as consistent in all aspects of his life as you can be.
- Replace his fear with something positive to do. To focus his mind, give him an easy task you have already taught, such as lowering his head.
- Use ropes long enough to allow drift so he feels less claustrophobic.
- Whenever possible, teach him new things at liberty so he can choose whether he wants to engage with the lesson.
- Use reward-based reinforcement to give him a focus other than his anxiety.

c) <u>What horses like this might find hard</u>:
- being calm when things get active
- yielding/disengaging hindquarters because he feels the need to be ready to flee
- facing you, as he finds face-to-face interaction worrying
- backing up - he wants to go forward at all costs
- learning confidence exercises - as he is often so anxious
- moving sideways because he'd rather go forward
- standing still - he hates having his forward movement blocked
- coming back in from work on a circle because he has to halt face-to-face.

3. Green - "Yeah, whatever, where's the grass?"

a) *Things to look for*: Most horses will show a few of these characteristics clearly, but not all of them. Any characteristic can show up as mild, moderate or strong.

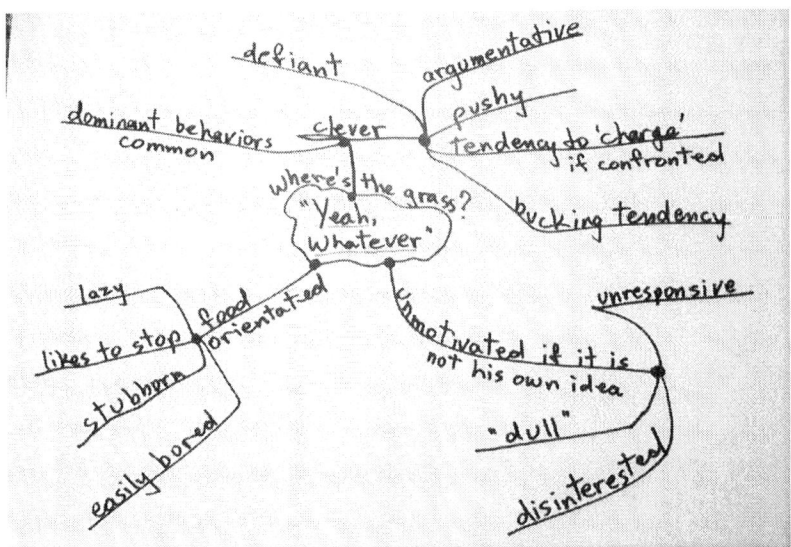

Figure 21: Characteristics of energy-conserving horses.

b) *Once you have his confidence* and his acceptance that you are higher than he is in the social order, this type of horse is usually curious, calm, dependable and tolerant.

Useful Training Concepts

- Providing motivation is the challenge with this type of horse.
- Give him a purpose that he can see; e.g., use of objects and obstacles to give obvious meaning to what we are asking the horse to do.
- Destinations at which he can stop; e.g., mats, nose targets, special grazing spots, particular places out on a ride or a walk.
- Keep a strong focus on the task at hand.
- Use reverse psychology to keep him from taking over.

- Move on to add new things to the repertoire as soon as he's ready.
- Take the time (i.e., repeated *short* sessions) needed to learn something well, but no 'drilling'.
- Use incentives such as food, rest, scratches (if he is highly social).
- Food-based reinforcement in the form of equine clicker training is the easiest way to reach his heart and mind.

c) <u>What horses like this might find hard</u>:
- motivation to do much at all
- yielding the forequarters as this is a submissive behavior
- coming to you
- more aloof horses may not like to be touched a lot
- circles with no variation
- maintaining gait and direction, especially in an arena situation
- interaction at liberty.

4. Blue Mood – "I'm worried about this!"

a) <u>Things to look for</u>: Most horses will show a few of these characteristics clearly, but not necessarily all of them. Any characteristic can show up as mild, moderate or strong.

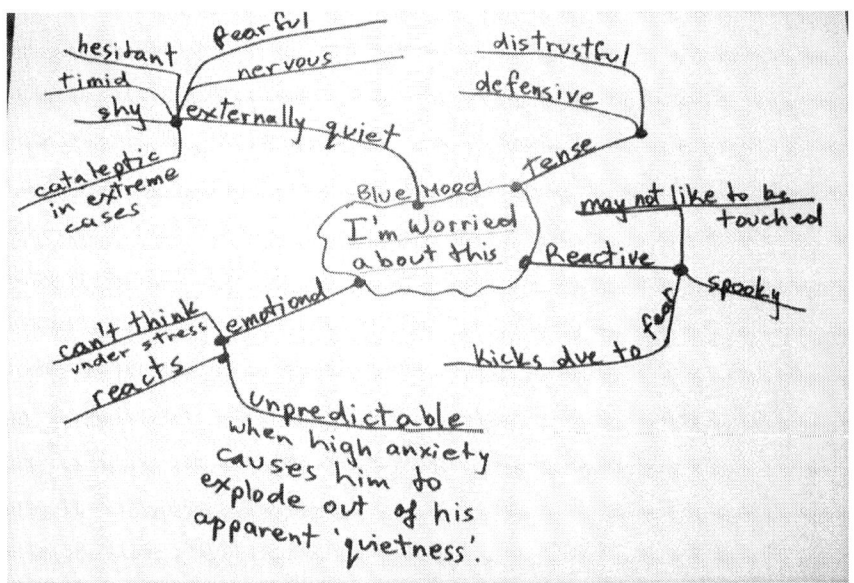

Figure 22: Characteristics of horses who internalize their anxiety and become 'stuck' when they don't understand what is wanted.

b) <u>Once you have his confidence</u>, this type of horse is usually sensitive, submissive, and obedient. They usually form a strong bond with a person they trust.

Useful Training Concepts

- These horses mainly seek comfort.
- Go slowly, don't push.
- Train with very small steps (extreme thin-slicing).
- Give lots of dwell time during lessons.
- Look for blinking and secret lip-licking: wait until it finishes.
- After a good effort, allow a long relaxing pause.
- Be super consistent.
- Do lots of repetition via *short* frequent specific lessons.
- Build confidence by guiding from behind the withers to ask him to put his nose on things.

- Spend lots of down time together. Share time and space with him by sitting in his home reading, meditating or gazing at the clouds.
- Reward-based reinforcement in the form of equine clicker training gives this type of horse a focus that helps over-ride his natural anxiety.

c) *What horses like this might find hard*:
- trusting people who are inconsistent and who increase pressure if the horse is stuck, instead of returning to where the horse can be confident
- moving or disengaging hindquarters
- facing you
- being sent away from you
- interacting at liberty.

Alongside these four horse character categories are two further characteristics that seem innately part of a horse's personality.

Self-Assertion

The first of these characteristics is what is sometimes called 'spirit'. Usually we think of a 'spirited' horse as one that moves easily with confidence. A horse that moves easily *without* confidence, due to fearfulness, is often called 'flighty'.

However, a "Yeah, whatever" type of horse, the sort whose main aim is seeking out the next blade of grass, may demonstrate a strong spirit to have his own way.

My horse, Boots, is confident and strong-willed. So although she is mostly an energy-conserving horse, she has a strong will or 'spirit' to make things fit with her own plans whenever an opportunity presents itself. If asked to do something, she likes to do a cost/benefit analysis before she makes up her mind.

I think *self-assertion* is a good term to explain this quality. Anyone with a toddler knows the moment self-assertion begins. Usually it is accompanied by the word, "No".

The way we view and go about raising children or training horses will define how we deal with a child or a horse when they say, "No".

Within any group of horses, people, dogs, pigs, sparrows – indeed any type of animal that naturally lives in a group, there will be some individuals who are strongly self-assertive and others who are less so. We can think of it as a continuum, with the strongly self-assertive at one end and those who really just want an easy life at the other end.

The more self-assertive a horse is, the more likely we'll see dominant behaviors directed at other horses and people that the horse considers lower in the social order. With captive horses, dominant behaviors show up most dramatically when a resource such as food is only available intermittently.

This is not the same as a horse who has learned, from interactions with people, that biting, kicking out or wheeling and running off are techniques that allow him to avoid things which cause him fear, anxiety or annoyance.

Such habits are usually created by faulty human reactions that cause the horse's oppositional responses to become self-motivating for the horse.

If a horse flattens his ears, causing the person about to touch his face to back off, the horse has learned a way to defend his personal space. The person is often totally unaware that as they backed off, they reinforced the horse's assertive expression.

Benefits of Strong Self-Assertion

Higher status in the group ensures greater influence and first dibs at the available resources. The purpose of human hierarchies (think class systems, business organisations, schools, hospitals, politics, and the military) is exactly the same.

When there is plentiful food and water, the more easy-going, less self-assertive horses (or people) fare well because they avoid conflict with other group members.

When food and water are in short supply, the most self-assertive horses (or people) will have the best chance of survival. When food is running out, the less assertive horses will sport bite marks on their butts and lose body condition faster than the more assertive-natured horses.

Researchers have noted that the offspring of assertive parents tend to also be assertive. So a foal born to a high-ranking mare will tend to maintain a relatively high rank through his or her life within the same or similar social grouping.

At the other end of the spectrum, a foal born to a less assertive mare will tend to remain at a relatively lower rank.

Since young horses learn mainly from the actions of their mother and other horses in their group, the makeup of an individual horse's character involves the usual mix of genetic input and learned behaviors - nature and nurture.

Foals that are kindly handled by people from birth will view those people as part of their extended family group and easily learn from them, if the teaching is appropriate.

Social Factor Continuum

The *Social Factor Continuum* is the second additional element that we need to consider when deciding how to best be with our horse. Horses on the *very social* end of the spectrum love to be touched and rubbed and enjoy being near you.

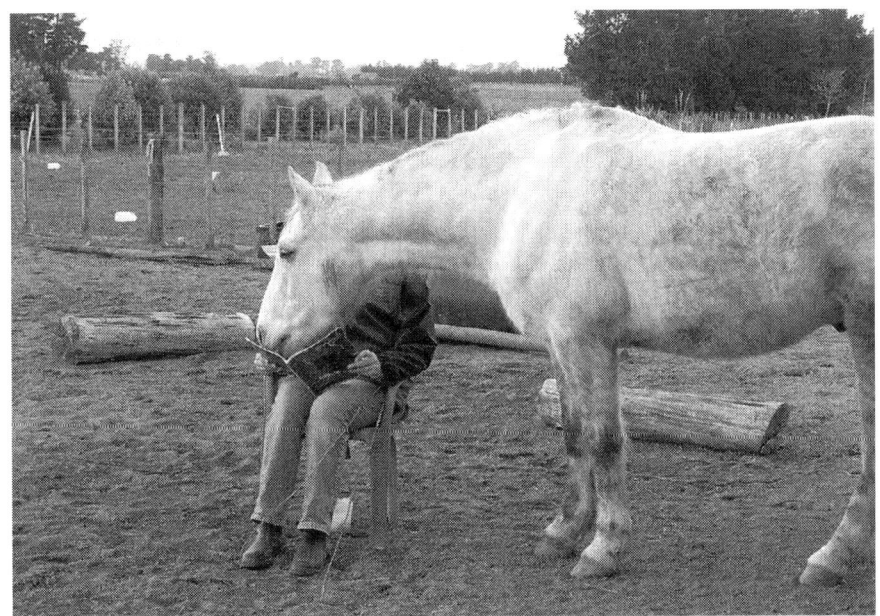

Figure 23: Smoky is a confident, "Where's the grass?" type of horse with a <u>low</u> self-assertion factor and a very <u>high</u> social factor. When sharing time and space with Smoky, he loves to stand close, nibble and lick. He adores being groomed.

Unlike the horse with a high social factor in Figure 23, *aloof* type horses are more 'distant' and don't seem to have a desire for lots of touchy-feely contact. They often don't enjoy grooming. When grooming is introduced carefully, aloof horses usually learn to tolerate it, but may never really like it.

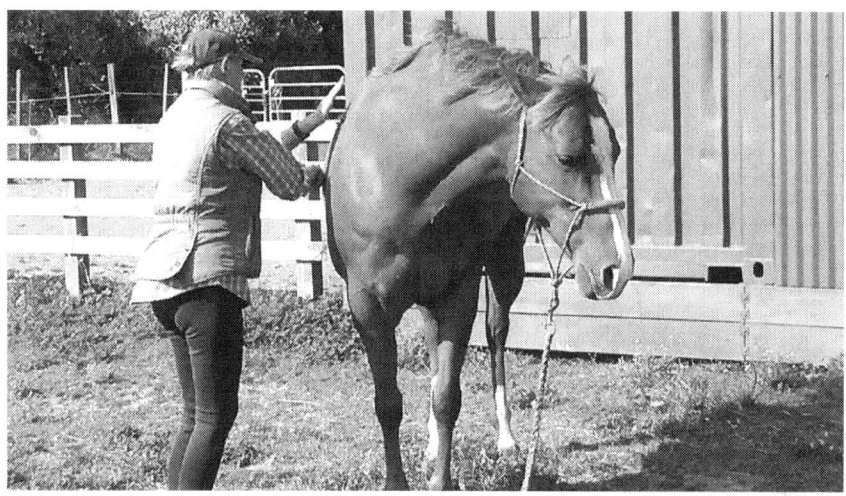

Figure 24: Boots is a confident, "Where's the grass?" type of horse with a <u>high</u> self-assertion factor and a <u>low</u> social factor. She often doesn't enjoy grooming but has learned to tolerate it during daily brushing in the summer months.

The Chameleon Inside Our Horse

It is not unusual for people to present different aspects of themselves in different situations. We may be forthright and in charge at work, but become completely mellow at home with our family.

We may behave quite differently when meeting new people as compared to how we behave with old friends. If we feel threatened, we may get belligerent or we may withdraw.

It is therefore not hard to understand that horses are the same. Their natural herd culture ensures that they develop strong kinship and friendship ties. When we bring them into our world they will form friendship bonds with us, if we prove ourselves worthy of their trust.

I highlight this point because building a positive relationship with a horse is similar to building a new relationship with another person. If the first contact with another person feels positive, you will set up more encounters to get to know the person better.

As time goes by, the relationship is sustained with continued positive interactions. Alternatively, the relationship dwindles away if you stop giving it your time and attention.

If we work with other people, we have to do our best to get along with them. Sometimes this is hard. Just as we often can't choose our workmates, so horses can't choose their 'person'.

If the horse is lucky, there will be one or more people 'at his job' who are sympathetic to his emotional, mental and physical needs. If he is unlucky, he will be forced into some sort of straightjacket.

To keep his 'job', he will have to seem to comply. If he doesn't comply enough, he will be 'moved on'.

Allowed sufficient time and positive experiences, a horse will usually build a willing relationship with a person. Even if the experiences are not so positive, a horse will habituate to consistent experiences. He has to, in order to survive.

For some reason, many people think that the positive willingness a horse shows with his trusted handler or owner should transfer to every other person. This doesn't really make sense. Such an expectation is the same as going to bed and finding that your husband has substituted another man in his place.

Some people may find this quite exhilarating, but others would be totally freaked out. (I suppose it depends on the confidence of the woman and the aptitude of her husband's stand-in.)

What I'm trying to say is that if you hand your horse, who trusts you, over to another person to handle or ride, you are suddenly thrusting the horse into a totally new situation.

If the other person is adept at reading horses and willing to adjust his behavior to what the horse requires, it can be a good experience.

If, however, the new person is working to their own agenda and speaks a different language than you use with your horse, you are putting the horse into a very awkward situation.

Your horse will also behave differently depending on where you are and what you are asking him to do. Horses are routinely faced with situations such as:

- being taken to a new place by a trusted person or an unknown person
- travelling in a known vehicle or an unknown vehicle
- being put in with unknown horses
- being put into isolation as in a stall
- being taken to a show or rally or clinic among lots of other stressed horses
- being taken onto unknown trails
- being left behind when his horse friends go out
- being taken away from home with his friends left behind.

There are many other situations. You could list the ones most relevant for your horse.

Your quiet, dependable horse at home can easily become an extremely anxious 'red alert' fellow in a new situation.

If we remain aware of this, it will be easier to retain our emotional neutrality and respond in a way that is most appropriate for the horse at that moment.

Giving the horse time and multiple opportunities to get used to a new situation is usually the fairest and safest thing to do.

Anxious type horses tend to be more timid, but also more compliant once they understand our signals. If we can keep them feeling comfortable, they are usually happy to follow our suggestions rather than challenge them.

Confident, imaginative type horses tend to be assertive rather than timid and may argue about what they are going to do next. They like to challenge our position in the social order, but it is not out of 'meanness' or 'being bad'. It is simply part of their bold, imaginative make-up. Such horses like to test the boundaries often.

Very aloof horses are often super-sensitive and it is easy to use signals that are too strong for them. As mentioned earlier, even when they are habituated to interaction with humans, they often don't like to be groomed. They may tolerate it with good grace, but they don't seek it out.

If we have an aloof horse, it is important to accept this as part of his character and not feel personally affronted because he is not touch-feely when we really would like to pet him like a cuddly toy.

The tendency toward being more social or more aloof is probably a combination of inborn characteristics and the influence of early environments.

If a horse's early environment did not allow for close interaction with friendly people he may appear aloof at first but change to become more social as he learns to trust you. Other horses will always tend to keep an emotional distance.

Hopefully this chapter helps give you a basis for observing and recording what you notice about your horse. It gives a terminology to use when we think and talk about different horse character types.

We have to remember that the characteristics within each category are on a sliding scale or continuum.

A horse's behavior in a particular situation is always a combination of his innate character, past experiences, the influences of the environment and what is happening at the moment.

Here is a mind map that describes my horse, Boots, in various situations.

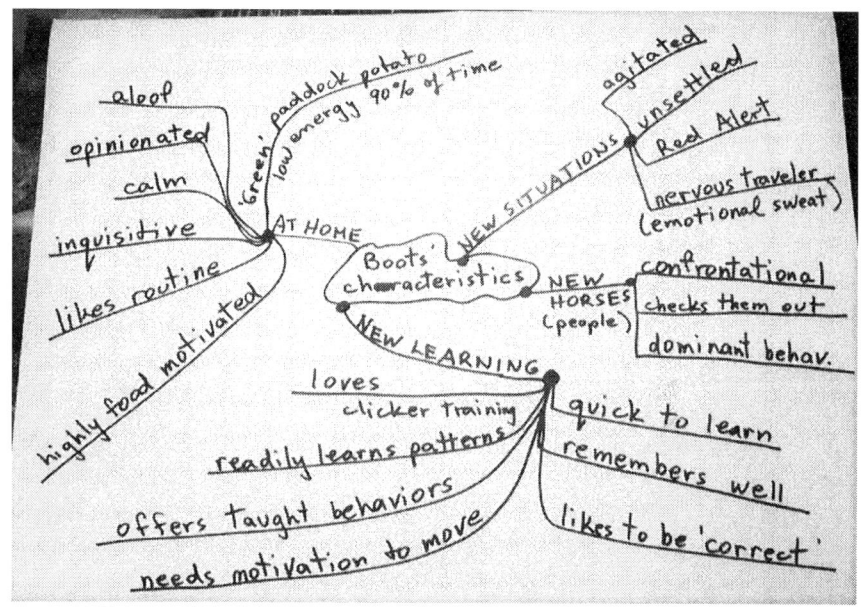

Figure 25: A mind map describing my horse, Boots.

Boots is three-quarters Quarter Horse, born in 2002 and has been in my care since she was 18 months old. For a while we traveled to other venues, but not enough to make her truly confident in new situations away from home in the presence of strange horses.

We spend time most days out and about in the neighborhood. She's always been happy to leave home for a walk or a ride, either with or without her paddock mate. It is a challenge to keep her weight down at a healthy level.

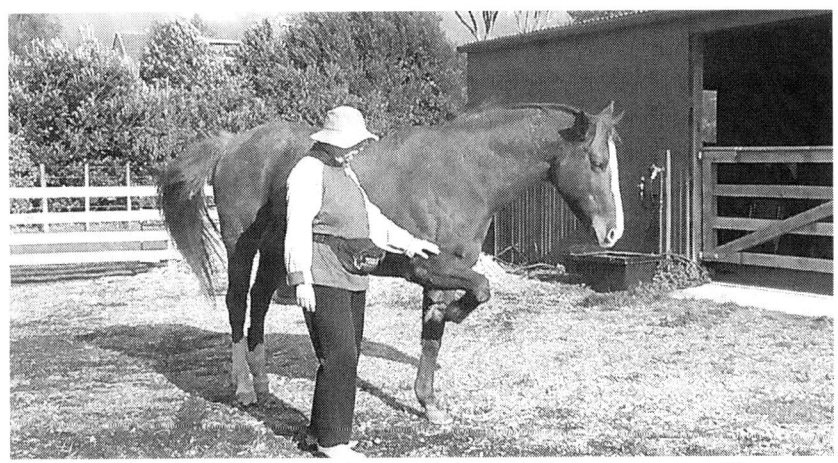

Figure 26: Boots enjoys clicker training games like 'leg lifts' to target my hand.

A mind map describing your horse's character type, as it presently appears to you, is a good addition to your Horse Folder. Be sure to put the date on all your documents so you can look back and compare changes over time.

Sending Horses Away for Training

People often underestimate how discriminating and sensitive horses are to human behavior. If a horse is sent away to a trainer, not only is his whole routine (including his diet) changed, but he has to adjust to the new establishment and the new trainer. Some horses seem to cope with this sort of change more easily than others.

When he goes home after his time with the trainer, chances are good that his owner or handler have not been part of the same training experience, yet the owner/handler may expect the horse to 'do' for him what he saw the horse 'do' for the trainer. If we think about this carefully, that is a totally unrealistic expectation.

Even with strong adherence to a specific training system, different people will approach the horse with different energy, different mannerisms, different behaviors, and different emotional states.

It's the adaptability of horses that helps them survive the peculiarities of human nature and human behavior.

The next chapter looks at the sorts of tools that are available for our horse training kitbag. One of the tools is a Horse Folder, in which we keep all the documents relating to our Training Plans and IEPs.

Chapter 4

What do we have in our Toolbox?

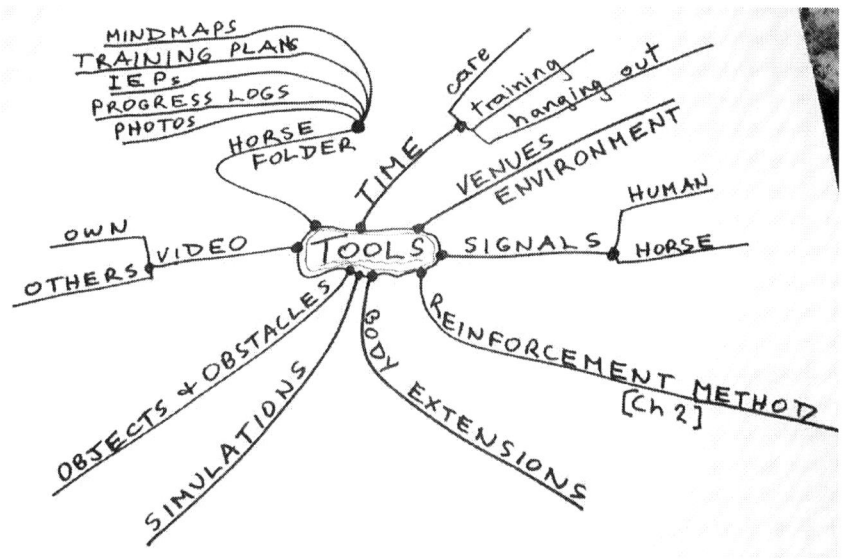

Figure 27: This is a mind map I did while considering the different tools that we can use to educate our horse.

When we begin writing a Training Plan, mind maps are useful. They become quick reminders about what we want to consider as we write our new Plan and IEP. Mind maps are great thinking tools for the following reasons.

- They encourage us to jot down ideas as they occur, without having to put them in any particular order or give them a value judgement.
- They are just ideas that we can add, delete and change.
- We can organise the ideas into new mind maps that we like better.
- Each idea can be put on a card (backs of cereal cartons make good cards) so we can move them around the

central theme of our mind map until they are in an arrangement that we like.
- Using different colors for each branch of a mind map helps the brain remember the relationships.

There are computerised mind mapping programs. Some of the basic ones are free. However, I find that drawing them by hand makes it easier to glance over them any time and make changes as they come to mind.

I like to ponder my mind maps for several days so my subconscious can play with the possibilities around each topic. An A3 sized pad or a big student project book are ideal for creating mind maps.

Each arm of the mind map can have multiple branches and sub-branches as we delve into more detail about the subject.

Once the key topics are set down on my first mind map (Figure 27), I develop mind maps to further break down each key topic. For example, Figure 28 looks at possible venues or environments where we can spend time with our horse.

Venues

Figure 28: The 'Venues/Environments' branch of my first mind map spawned two branches which in turn give rise to a large number of possibilities.

The venues we have available obviously play a big part in our Training Plans and Individual Education Programs.

Boots and I are fortunate in having small pens, a fenced arena with an all-weather surface, various grazed paddocks (depending on time of year), grassy paddocks, a covered space the size of a roomy stall, roads with minimal traffic, a couple of farm tracks, and a driveway.

Figure 29: We have a large river reserve within walking distance. We play there when the dairy cows are absent.

We have puddles in the winter and I also have hills and a few slopes to work with. Luckily these are all within walking distance because my horse trailer was sold to afford our all-weather arena surface. I can set up a temporary round or square pen if I want to use one.

Mind map your venues

A good start to general planning might be to create a mind map of all the venues which you can access. Once you start looking around and contemplating sites, there may be more than you first thought.

A 'venues' mind map is a useful reference when you want to plan (1) the best place to first introduce a new task, (2) places to practice to get the task fluid, and (3) new locations where you can generalize the task.

- If you are in a public boarding facility, what venues can you use and when is each one available to you?
- If you have roads, when is there least traffic?

- Which venues are within walking distance?
- Do you find it easy to transport your horse to other venues?
- Do you generally train alone or do you have a training buddy?
- Do you have a quiet training environment or is it always busy with other people and horses?
- Can you have your horse's buddies in view but not able to interfere with your training?
- Are there places you will be able to use once you and/or your horse become more confident?

Other venues not included in Figure 28 are showgrounds, farms and race tracks. At our former home, we could walk or trailer to the local showgrounds and play with all sorts of extra facilities.

Time

The time you have available to work, play, ride or relax with your horse obviously has a large influence on your Plan and IEP.

If your horse lives with you and you take care of him yourself, training usually meshes nicely with everyday care. Even if you only have a few minutes, you can use them to play with the current slice of your latest IEP. Horses learn well with short but frequent bursts of focused teaching and learning.

If your horse lives elsewhere, you have to factor in the handling styles of the people who look after your horse in your absence. He may be in a paddock with a herd, in which case handling by others may be minimal.

He may be handled daily by several people. Horses are well aware that people and other horses come in a variety of character types. They know that they may have to behave in a certain way with this person and in a different way with that person.

Each person brings an individual aura of energy plus certainty or uncertainty. Horses used to being around people read people in the same way as they read other horses.

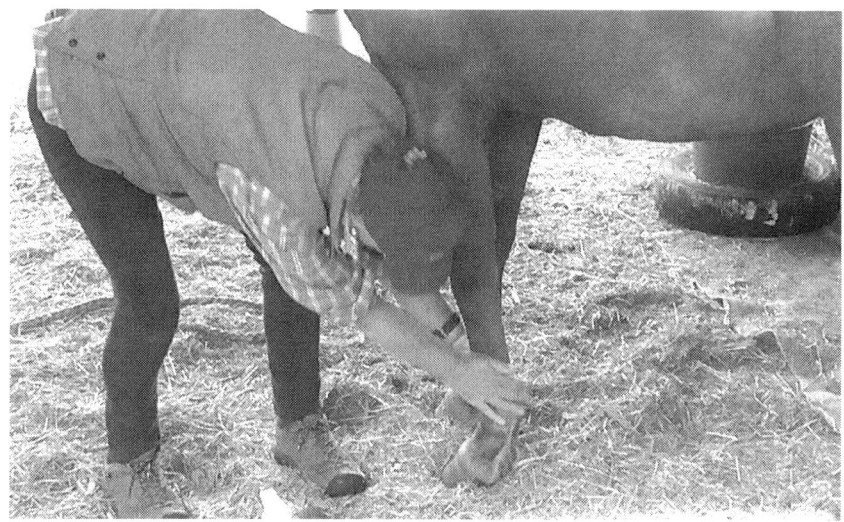

Figure 30: Your horse may at times be in the care of other people. Bridget is massaging Boots' legs. Boots is relaxed even though Bridget is not a regular visitor. Horses instantly recognize the energy and aura of a different person, as well as their level of confidence around a horse.

As long as you work consistently with your horse, he will recognize what you do with him as 'your way'. As long as you are fair and dependable, he will play your games with your rules.

It's ideal if the other people looking after your horse communicate the same way you do, but it is not always possible to find the ideal boarding facility.

The time that other people spend with your horse, and what they do with him, is a factor to consider in your Training Plans and IEPs.

Obviously the less frequently you are able to be with your horse, the longer it will take to achieve an IEP. But achieve it you will. Horses seem to contemplate what we are teaching them when we are not there.

I've found that if I've taught something well, with really good thin-slicing, the horse remembers it years later, even if it is not something we do very often.

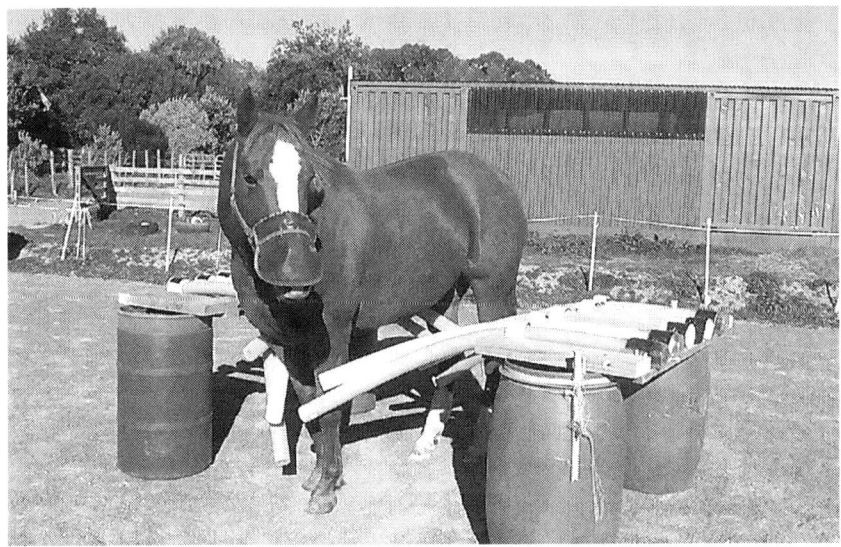

Figure 31: We learned about walking through five pairs of pool noodles about six months ago. When they show up again in a Horse Agility course, Boots is keen to play. During summer she wears a sun shield to stop her nose from burning badly.

A clip called <u>Thin Slicing the Pool Noodle Task</u> in my *Thin-Slicing Examples* playlist illustrates the Training Plan used with Boots to build her confidence with this strange request.

Simulations

When we write a new Training Plan, there may be simulations we can include to make the teaching and learning easier.

Having another person stand in for the horse is a huge help. It allows us to experiment with, and practice, our body language and rope handling skills without confusing the horse while we work things out in our own mind and muscles.

The 'horse' person can also give us clear feedback by telling us how our actions and attitude feel to them.

Simulations without the horse

1. We can walk patterns with a 'pretend' horse or a person standing in for the horse. I find this especially useful when I am setting up ten different obstacles for the monthly Horse Agility course.
2. There are many exercises we can do to improve our rope and body extension handling skills.
3. We can practice body language skills such as clear 'walk on' and 'halt' multi-signals. When we practice with a person we can get useful feedback about how our signals and body language feel to the person.
4. We can learn and practice how to handle a lead rope with finesse. We can tie the halter to a fence or loop it over a door so that the lead rope attaches at horse height. This gives us opportunity to get good at running our hand or fingers up the rope as gently as possible.

Figure 32: Simulations: we can hang our halter on a fence or door at horse height and practice mechanical details.

In Figure 32 I am reaching across my body to gently run my fingers up the rope. This is my signal for asking the horse to back up while I am facing him. I want the movement of my hand along the rope to be smooth and in my muscle memory.

5. Simulations are great for getting adept with long-reins. It is an interesting learning experience to long-rein a person holding a halter in front of themselves in two hands, to mimic the horse's head. They can give us clear feedback about how our long-rein signals feel to them. Are they clear and, distinct or are we sending a lot of 'static' down the line?

6. It is even more interesting to have different people drive you on long-reins. The difference in the 'feel' of different people is astounding. Since horses notice everything, this is a real eye-opener.

Simulations with the horse

Trailer loading is a good example of a context where simulations are priceless. Trailer loading is one of the life skills every horse needs. Even if we don't have a trailer and never intend to take the horse anywhere he can't walk, things can happen to us, or the horse.

We may have to evacuate due to flood or fire or noxious fumes. The horse may need to get to a vet clinic. If he is sold or re-homed, he will usually have to travel.

Trailer loading has many aspects we can address with mini-simulations. There are two DVDs in my DVD & Notes set called *Trailer Loading* (listed in the 'Further Resources' section). A large portion of the DVD footage deals with a range of pre-requisites or 'mini-skills' that we can teach to prepare our horse to load up with minimal concern.

By playing with all the mini-skills in a variety of places, trailer loading loses much of its trauma because the *horse and handler have forged a mutual language* and trust about approaching, entering and exiting small spaces.

We can simulate many of the things we want the horse to learn, for example:

- walking up a ramp using a slope
- backing down a ramp using a slope
- walking down a ramp using a slope (Figure 33)
- putting up the butt bar by teaching the horse to back his butt against a safe fence or a tree (Figure 34)
- stepping onto unusual trailer surfaces by teaching the horse to walk over tarps, mats and boards
- asking the horse to walk into the trailer space on his own while we stay at the 'ramp', using a dead-end lane as our 'trailer' (Figure 35)
- making clanking trailer noises by tapping items and wiggling chains
- making external trailer noises by tagging the trailer with a stick&string or lunging whip while the horse is with us outside the trailer
- standing quietly in a trailer by teaching the horse to 'park' with his front feet on a destination mat (away from the trailer) and gradually increase the time he stays 'parked' (Figure 36)
- staying parked in a narrow, trailer-like space
- the handler disappearing out of sight after the horse is loaded by teaching him to stay 'parked' for longer and longer before we reappear after 'disappearing' behind a visual barrier. #18 *HorseGym with Boots* illustrates a way of doing this.
- moving 'one step at a time' in a variety of situations so we can negotiate quiet entrances into and exits out of a trailer
- 'stepping up' and 'stepping down' using a pedestal in case the trailer does not have a ramp (Figure 37)
- the solid sides of a trailer by covering the sides of our simulation trailer with sheets or tarps.

#74 HorseGym with Boots is a video clip showing how we started with the frame for a box with withers-high sides,

and gradually added sides and front to close it in on three sides to resemble a horse trailer.

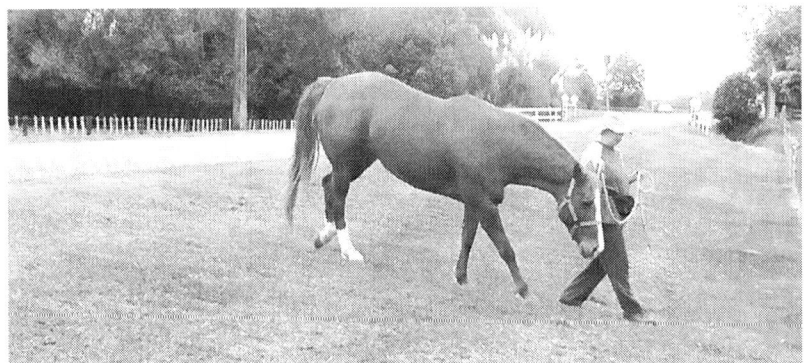

Figure 33: We can use a slope to get the horse comfortable with walking down a ramp, up a ramp as well as backing down a ramp.

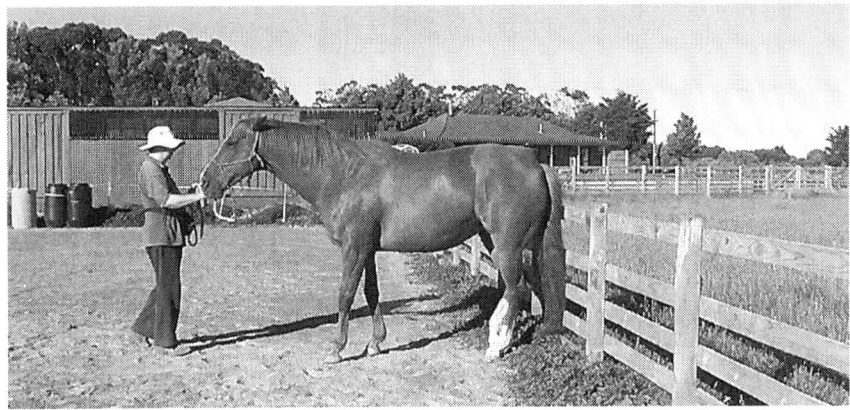

Figure 34: Teaching the horse to put his butt against a safe barrier helps prepare him for having the butt bar put up in a trailer. We can use barrels, trees, walls, hedges and the outside of a horse trailer to generalize the idea.

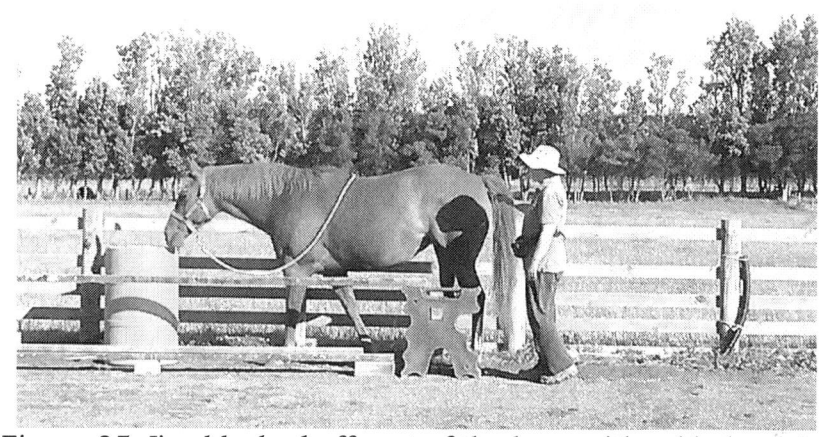

Figure 35: I've blocked off part of the lane with a big barrel to make a space the size of a trailer bay. I've stayed at the back of the 'trailer' simulation, tossed the rope over her back and asked Boots to 'load up' by herself.

Figure 36: Boots is learning to 'stay parked' in her 'trailer' until further notice. We can build up this skill one second at a time until the horse can confidently wait for a full minute. The next stage is to have the horse stay relaxed in the 'trailer' while we move out of sight. We'd start with disappearing for one second, and gradually make it longer, coming back after each interval for a click&treat.

Figure 37: Zoe is asking Boots to step four feet up onto a pedestal and then step down backwards to simulate a step-in trailer.

If the horse and handler already have a strong mutual language to accomplish the tasks above, it only remains to apply them to a trailer. If the horse is comfortable with using all sorts of objects and obstacles, the trailer will be just one more object and obstacle to play with.

If we use the outside of the trailer for all sorts of activities, the horse is likely to see finally getting into the trailer as a chance to have a lovely rest. The clip called <u>Single Obstacle Challenges, The Trailer</u> in my *Single Obstacle Challenges* playlist, shows a way that Boots and I played with our trailer as an object. Actually going into the trailer was only a small part of the overall session.

As well as the individual tasks already listed, we can set up trailer simulations as in Figures 35 and 36. The simulations serve to teach us and the horse various aspects of trailer loading.

Trailer loading problems mostly arise due to one or both of the following reasons.

1. The horse has not been carefully taught all the small individual skills that make up the big task of loading and unloading. Entering a narrow space on wheels is way too overwhelming as a single task for an animal who, to feel safe, depends on the ability to scan the open horizon and a rapid flight response.
2. The handler has not yet carefully learned how to teach and guide the horse through all the small individual steps that make up the big task of loading and unloading. They have not yet developed a mutual language for each step of the process.

Handlers often approach trailer loading with trepidation and uncertainty simply because they have not yet had the opportunity to master all the small slices that could bring them seamlessly to loading up with confidence.

Horses pick up a negative human emotion such as anxiety in a heartbeat. When the horse realizes that his human buddy is feeling unsure about this 'trailer' situation, he is instinctively going to be unsure as well.

Therefore, it is important to do everything we can to make *ourselves* comfortable and accurate with each aspect of trailer loading. Ideally, we use a person to stand in for the horse. If we have access to a horse who is calm and comfortable about trailer loading, we can play with him to gain confidence and improve our technique and reduce our perfectly natural anxiety.

A human stand-in for the horse is always a good starting point because it allows us to practice the body positions, signals and rope handling skills we'll use to send the horse into the trailer and ask him out again.

Be sure to take a turn to be the horse and ask a novice to load you up. If you can, also ask an experienced horse handler to load you up and note how each one feels.

Trailer loading is one example of a context for simulation exercises. With creative thought, we can come up with simulations for many of the things we want to teach.

Another useful planning resource is drawing up a mind map of all the simulations you can think of, and add to it as new thoughts occur.

Objects and Obstacles

A paddock or arena with no objects and obstacles limits the games we can play with our horse. It also limits gymnastic exercises other than using the boundary fence and corners. Objects and obstacles let us set up lots of activities that make sessions more interesting for the horse and the handler.

If we are in a round pen, even the corners are missing, although it can be fun to use both the inside and the outside of a round pen. We can put objects inside or outside the round pen to create a circuit of tasks, using the round pen barrier to deflect the horse's energy.

If our available training venues are limited, adding objects and obstacles immediately adds interest and possibilities.

Even a simple set of obstacles and objects can be rearranged in many different ways to set up fresh challenges. Here are a few things that are not too hard or expensive to collect.

Possible Arena Obstacles

- trotting poles (wooden rails or plastic pipe) for gymnastic hock flexion, rhythm and tempo
- rails for backing over or sidestepping along
- pedestals for stepping up and stepping down
- sheets or blankets for confidence with covers put on and slipping off
- barrels for bending around, weaving through, backing up against, jumping over, side-passing along, or rolling
- cones as destinations, for weaving and for marking out shapes
- tarps for confidence with unusual surfaces

- curtains or pool noodles for pushing through
- small jumps for leaping over
- scary corridors of flags or bunting for walking, trotting and cantering through
- lanes made of rails for precise leading positions and halts
- mats as destinations

Figure 38: It's good to know that our horse can be cool and calm with something like a sheet fluttering in the wind and blowing off in a gale.

Figure 39: Different horses have different ways of getting confident with new surfaces. Pawing is a way horses gain information about the nature of a surface. Horses will often paw water or trailer ramps to find out if the surface is safe to stand on. It's important to let them paw until they have satisfied themselves that it is safe. Unshod horses can feel a great deal through their hoof wall.

Figure 40: A combination of curtain and jump for a Horse Agility competition.

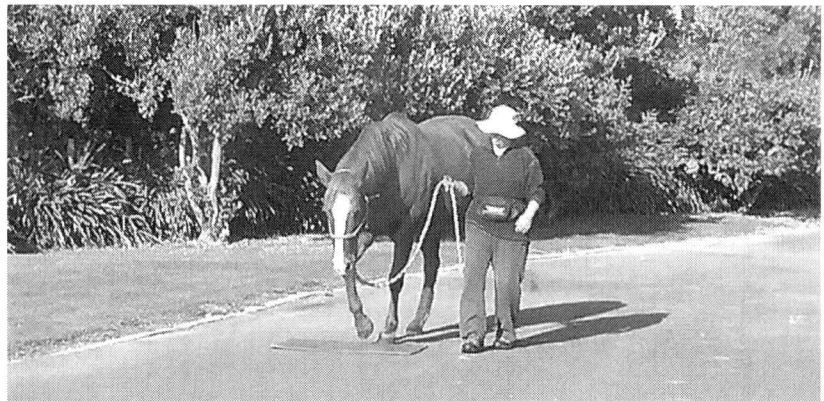

Figure 41: Like humans, horses gain confidence by knowing what is going to happen before it happens. Boots knows she will come to a halt on the mat, so she is able to prepare her mind and body for the halt. Our venue here is a driveway.

- nose targets (plastic bottles or rags) for destinations
- umbrellas for confidence with something opening out and hovering overhead
- bouncing balls for confidence with unusual movements
- big balls for confidence with something big and unusual rolling around the horse's legs and put on his back
- balls for nudging, kicking or chasing

Figure 42: This is a 'treat ball'. It comes apart so it can be filled with horse pellets that come out of the hole when the horse rolls the ball around.

#25 HorseGym with Boots looks at playing with a big ball to build confidence with unusual movement and having a large strange thing on the horse's back (which may at times be you).

Natural Obstacles

- hills and slopes
- trees
- overhanging bushes
- stumps
- gates
- white lines on roads
- road signs
- mailboxes
- tractors, trucks, cars, bikes, joggers, baby buggies
- narrow places
- logs

Figure 43: Natural obstacles give us new and interesting challenges.

- gullies, ditches
- bridges
- streams, ponds, lakes, ocean
- puddles.

Figure 44: Horses have poor depth perception and are extremely careful about where they put their feet. This makes them wary about stepping into water if they are unsure about the surface below. With careful thin-slicing we can help a horse gain confidence with water in different situations.

If you are going to write a Training Plan and IEP for water confidence, a video example with Smoky, called *Water & Tarp Obstacle*, can be found in my *Thin-slicing Examples* playlist.

If you don't have barrels to play with, a set of big cardboard boxes is an option. If you collect boxes that fit inside each other, they will be easy to store and transport, although not so good in the wet or wind.

If you don't have cones, plastic bottles of water make good markers. Five-litre containers are especially useful. The cleaner at your local school probably gets materials in containers of a nice size and may be pleased to rehome them when they are empty. I've used rocks, blocks of firewood and rags as markers.

Bottles, containers and rags can be set end-to-end to make a 'rail' or a small jump. A tarp rolled up can also stand in as a rail.

If you don't have rails, hoses and ropes can be arranged into shapes on the ground such as:

- lanes (straight or curved)
- L-bends
- U-bends
- S-bends
- Z-bends.

Shapes like this give us a structure for learning and practicing signals for accurate foot placement.

Objects and obstacles allow us to set up interesting conversations with our horse. They can be things we come across during an outing, or things we collect for use in our training areas.

Body Extensions

American horseman Franklin Levinson says, "It is not any piece of equipment (tool) that is cruel or damages the horse; it is the human using it. Their lack of wisdom and knowledge, their inappropriate attitudes and beliefs and their unlearned and unpracticed skills that are the things that hurt and damage the horse". There is a link to his work in the Reference List at the end of the book.

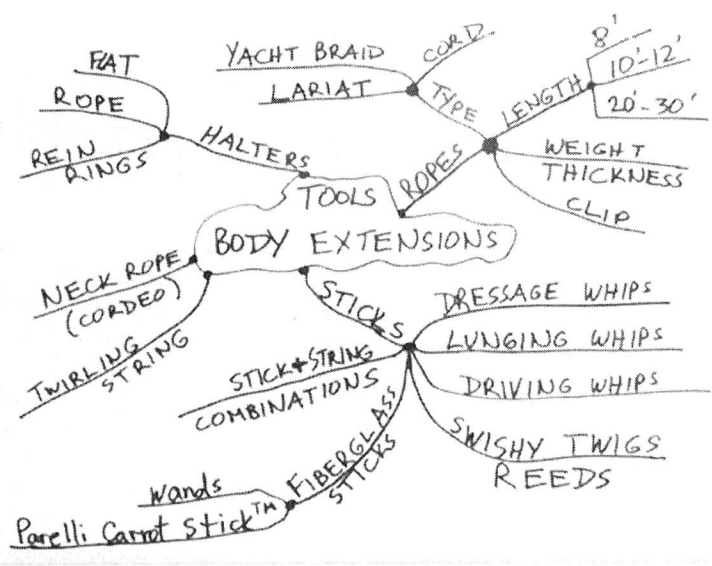

Figure 45: Used well, these tools don't become problems.

Because of our odd, upright shape, horses find it easier to read our intent if we carry a body extension to make our signals clearer. As long as we are consistent and mindful about how we use our body extensions, the horse accepts them as part of our normal body and body language.

Halter and Lead Ropes

It's possible to teach a horse to move along with us at liberty, using the click&treat dynamic.

Once the horse understands our signals for 'walk on' and 'halt', we can add the halter and rope. Doing it this way allows the halter and lead rope to morph into a way of holding hands rather than an instrument of restriction.

A clip called *Shadow Me Game at Liberty* can be found in my *Thin-Slicing Examples* playlist.

Some clicker trainers like to teach leading by having the horse follow a target taped to the end of a light stick. Once the horse responds to a voice signal for 'walk on' and 'halt', the target can be faded out.

Confidence with halter and lead is probably one of the most important skills we can teach our horse.

#65 HorseGym with Boots looks at a way of re-teaching, teaching or improving haltering using clicker training.

The Training Plan for haltering that accompanies Clip #65 appears later in this chapter as Example One in the *Clicker Training Logs* section.

Since our horse lives in a human-designed environment, we have no option other than to get him comfortable with halter and lead. Even if we only play with our horse at liberty in his paddock, at some point he will need to be moved from A to B through unfenced areas and with unusual distractions en route.

Horses trained carefully will respond to halter and rope as a guidance system which gives them security and information about what we would like them to do next.

Horses traumatised with halters and ropes do their best to avoid them and have learned resistance techniques. They need a detailed IEP that allows them to see the halter as a positive thing. We can teach them to see the rope as a conduit that sends gentle text messages to their head via the halter.

I use a variety of body extensions. Which one depends on what we are doing. When I do an Agility Course at liberty, I don't use any of them once Boots understands the pattern.

The *July 2015 clip* from my *2015 Horse Agility* playlist shows an Agility course done at liberty.

We may have a halter and lead or a bridle and reins on our horse, but that doesn't mean we have to put constant pressure on them. They can be in neutral most of the time as we focus on communicating our intent to the horse with body language and breathing.

Figure 46: Boots and I are practicing walking together with me beside her butt (Leading Position 5). The rope and stick are in neutral.

If body extensions are correctly introduced, the horse responds to them as he would to the neck, head, teeth, ears, tail, front feet and hind feet of another horse. Most of the time they are in neutral. They are only activated to clarify a message.

Walking on the road I use a halter and a long rope and carry a fibreglass stick. I use the rope to send text messages as needed and the stick makes a good walking stick.

If something unusual happens out on the road, the rope is long enough to allow the horse to drift, and the stick enables me to give clear signals to keep everyone safe. The *unusual* has happened about five times in the last two years during which time we have gone out and about in the neighborhood almost every day.

The first time we had an unusual experience, I had only a 12-foot rope and no stick. The incident was unexpected and involved other highly energized horses. I was experienced enough to keep everyone safe, but it highlighted how much easier such incidents are to manage if I simply use a long light lunge rein and carry a stick when we are walking out. We share the road with other walkers, baby buggies, motorbikes, tractors, juggernauts, dogs, cattle and other horses.

Sticks & Swinging Ropes

Figure 47: The first thing we have to establish with a stick is total confidence and comfort about being rubbed all over with it. In this photo, there is no intent in my body language other than to rub the stick on all over Boots. She reads my intent from my body language and works out what the stick means.

Sticks and their companion stick&string combinations and 'flags' made with a cloth or plastic bag on the end of a stick, used mindfully, allow us to make our intent clearer for the horse.

When sticks are used in a punishing way, rather than mindfully to clarify our requests, we can end up with a traumatized horse who becomes anxiously reactive as soon as he sees a stick-like object in the hands of a person. Most likely, a stick on the ground will not get the same response.

So it's not the stick itself that causes turmoil. It is the possible action and intent of the person holding the stick that causes the problem.

Figure 48: I'm using the stick mindfully to ask Boots to take a step or two back. I could use my hand, but if I want to stay shoulder-to-shoulder with the horse, the stick makes it easy to give a very light and clear signal. The stick is simply an extension of my body. Boots is reading my intent and in this photo she has realized that the stick is part of a signal, along with my voice and body language, asking her to step backwards.

There are groups of people who claim all sticks are innately evil and anyone using a stick to help educate a horse is either a bad person or has yet to 'see the light'.

Like most extremist views, this one is not helpful in real life. Sticks, used thoughtfully, can help horses learn required behaviors because the signals we can give with a stick are more horse-like than we can achieve with our strange, upright, two-legged body.

Essentially, a stick can make us more horse-like by acting like another horse's neck, teeth, front leg and hind leg. If we add a string to the stick, it can act like another horse's tail. Swinging the end of a rope also becomes a 'tail movement' signal.

We can swing the end of a rope mildly, moderately or strongly, depending on the situation. We can use the end of a rope to give a minimal signal or we can use it to tag the horse.

Such a tag resembles a mild bite from another horse. It happens once and is not repeated if the horse moves away. These are all actions horses innately understand because they correspond to species-specific body language communication between horses.

If a horse comes from a background that has made him worried about sticks or swinging ropes, the first challenge is to set up a careful IEP that allows him to form a new viewpoint.

Rather than avoiding his concern by not using a stick or a swinging rope, we can help make him more resilient by teaching him that sticks and ropes can give him useful information.

We want to change a horse's *reactions* to stick or rope pressure into *responses* to stick or rope pressure. Such training will enable the horse to understand a greater variety of actions carried out by the different people he may come across.

Figure 49: When there is no intent in our body language, the horse learns that there is no intent in the stick or the string or the rope being tossed over his body. We have to teach horses to read the intent behind the body extension. The body extension itself is a neutral item. Boots has <u>learned</u> to be 'actively inactive' while I gently toss the string all over her body. She is fairly relaxed but alert to what I'm doing.

Standing Still Willingly

It's up to us to teach a horse the response of standing still when we don't want him to move while we rub him with a stick or toss a string/rope over his back.

Standing still during commotion is not something a horse would ever do naturally. A horse's instinctive response is to move away until he feels safe enough to review the situation. If he decides that maybe it's not dangerous, he will carefully come closer to satisfy his curiosity.

Once a new object is accepted as not dangerous, horses see it as part of the furniture as long as it stays in the same position. In other words, anxiety is tempered with curiosity and acceptance, so that the horse is not in a perpetual state of worry about everything.

Exactly the same dynamic underpins our own behavior. The unfamiliar makes us anxious. Then we become curious and in 'learning mode'. Finally, we feel comfortable in the new situation. After a recent move to a new part of the country, I was both anxious and curious about where everything was.

I was anxious and curious about working out the best routes to get to the places we needed to go. Now, two years later, the curiosity about most places is satisfied and the anxiety is reduced, unless I have to drive somewhere on an unfamiliar route.

Back to horses. As already mentioned, it's up to us to teach the horse to be 'actively inactive' in situations where we need him to stand still. A lot of people simply cross-tie their horse rather than take the time to teach 'active inaction'. A cross-tied horse has his options removed, and is forced to accept being helpless.

A horse carefully taught to be 'actively inactive' is much nicer to be around for haltering and bridling, grooming, saddling and unsaddling, mounting, dismounting, ground-tying, massage, foot care, hosing, traveling, vet care and so on.

#20 HorseGym with Boots looks at the importance of teaching 'standing still'.

As mentioned earlier, a large part of the process of learning to willingly stand still is the horse learning to read the intent behind a stick or swinging rope. We don't want the horse anxious about the items themselves.

#22 and *#24 HorseGym with Boots* look at teaching relaxation with ropes.

If we carry the stick much of the time, the horse sees it as a body part that we can use expressively when the need arises, in the same way as another horse activates his neck, head, tail and legs.

If we toss the rope all over his body with no intent in our body language for him to move, we are teaching a 'standing still' game with commotion.

Stick or Rope Intent

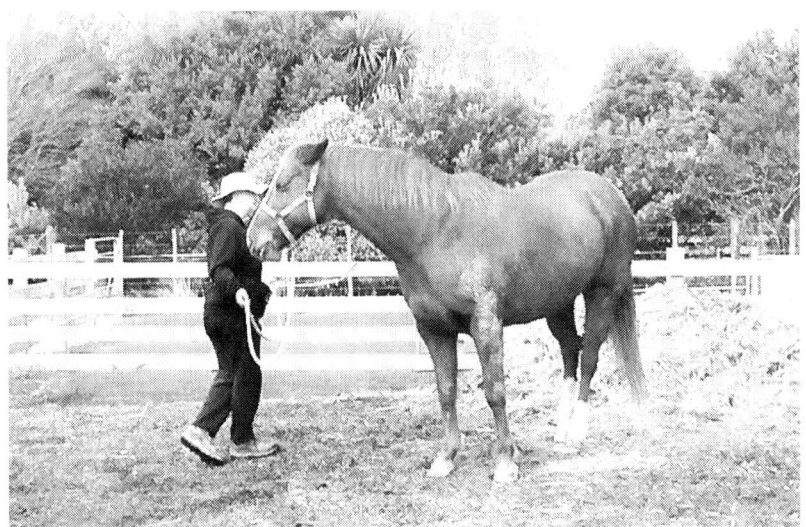

Figure 50: Swinging the end of the rope toward the hindquarters with intent in my body language gives Boots a clear signal that I would like her to yield her hindquarters away from me.

In Figure 50, Boots is about to move her left hind leg to take a step to the left in order to yield to the signal pressure. If we don't teach our horse basic appropriate responses to the pressures commonly used by people, we are not giving him the resilience he needs to understand what different people expect him to do.

Our rope can be in neutral, or we can swing the end of it to indicate that we would like the horse to yield his hindquarters away from the rope energy. The rope message may be pronounced when we first teach this signal, but as the horse comes to understand our intent, the signal easily becomes body language such as a small hand gesture toward the hindquarters. The rope is no longer needed.

Since we can't know who may be handling our horse in the future, it will make his life much easier if we carefully teach him appropriate responses to pressure applied in various ways – with sticks and ropes as well as hand touch and gestures. If we use reward reinforcement for the teaching process, horses quickly pick up the meaning of each type of signal.

If we rely only on free-shaping and reward reinforcement for all our teaching, we won't have a horse who is resilient in the wider world.

If we regularly carry our stick and make clear suggestions with the end of a rope as gently as we can, the horse sees these as part of our normal body language. Sticks allow us to communicate more clearly. Ropes are for sending polite text messages. Pulling, jerking, hitting and whipping are not a part of any plan or program.

Signal Awareness

The large topic of signals and cues is explored in my book, *Conversations with Horses: An In-depth look at Signals & Cues between Horses and Handlers.*

Figure 51 is a mind map that summarises signals used by people to communicate with horses.

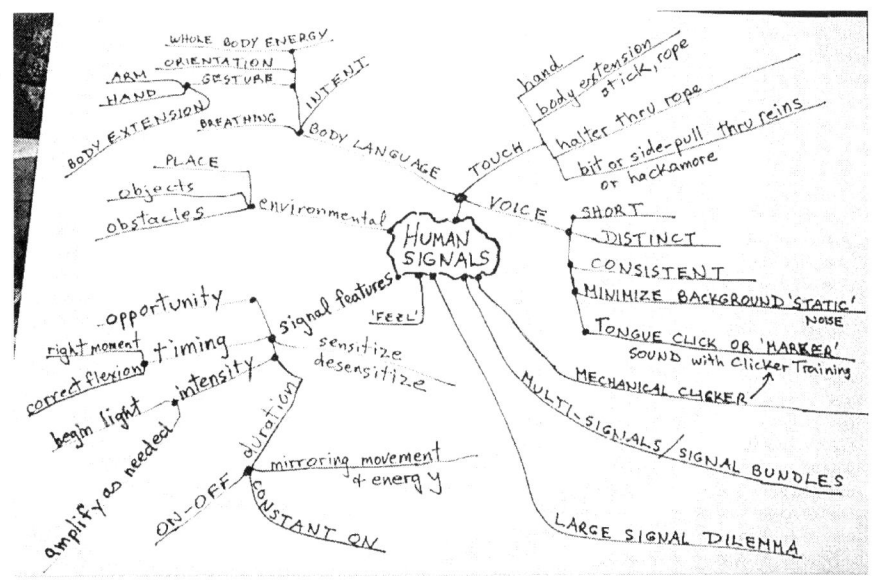

Figure 51: These signals are examined in detail in my book: 'Conversations with Horses: An In-depth look at Signals & Cues between Horses and Handlers'.

In this book, I will only comment on two of the branches that appear in Figure 51. The first is the *sensitize/desensitize* branch.

Sensitization and Desensitization

When we communicate with our horse, we are teaching him which things we'd like him to ignore (desensitization) and to which things he should pay attention (sensitization).

If we are teaching him to wear a saddle or harness, we want him desensitized to the feel and discomfort of the girth. Our Training Plan would include strategies to add good vibes to wearing a saddle. We could saddle up, feed the horse and then unsaddle him.

Or we could saddle up and take him for a walk to an especially nice grazing spot. When we've done things like this for several sessions (minimum of eight), we can increase the desensitization by doing all our ground work and walking out together wearing the saddle or harness.

If we are long-reining our horse we want him desensitized to the feel of the rope or reins along his side or legs, but we want him sensitized to the rein signals on his head-gear.

The other branch of Figure 51 that I want to consider is the *large signal dilemma* branch. The section that follows is a short piece from my book, *Conversations with Horses*.

Large Signal Dilemma

It's important that we don't get stuck in the 'large signal dilemma'. Sometimes people find a large signal that works and habitually use it forever to shout at the horse. They never think of developing the signal into a small whisper to give the same message.

Such handlers can help their horses by focusing on developing feel. Every horse will feel different. (*Conversations with Horses* has a section about developing 'feel').

Once we activate a rope or rein signal, 'feel' comes into play, allowing us to release our pressure the instant the horse softens to the pressure.

We close our hands or fingers slowly *to give the horse time to feel the pressure coming*, then we open our hands quickly the moment we can feel him responding to our pressure.

This release of pressure is the only way horses have of knowing what it is we want them to do. If we also use Clicker Training, the click is simultaneous with the release and the treat is offered immediately (ideally within three seconds).

If we release (or click) at the wrong time, the horse will not understand what we want.

'Feel' is inseparable from good timing. We have to be able to feel the moment we should release.

The video clip called *Thin-slice Soft Yield to Rein Signals* from my *Developing Soft Rein Response* playlist gives a good demonstration, especially from time mark 4:48, of how easily bad timing can confuse a horse.

If our feel for the timing of the release is faulty, we are dropping the horse into a cauldron of confusion. Some horses will try to fill in as best they can. Others may shut down and stop trying. Others again, will become energized with anxiety and want to move their feet to get away from a situation they don't understand.

A handler with a good sense of feel will know which of the above is happening, and adjust his training to bring the horse back to a place of confidence to try again, which might be on another day.

When horses put pressure on each other, the pressure goes away as soon as one horse moves away. In the wild there are obviously no ropes or artificial barriers that stop a horse from moving away. He gets instant release reinforcement. That is what good trainers seek to emulate. 'Feel' and timing are totally interrelated.

When we do ground work with halter and lead, we are holding hands via the rope. Alongside the rope signals, the horse is noticing our body orientation, our body energy, our gestures and maybe our touch to help him work out what we want.

That all changes as soon as the handler mounts up. When we ride, we suddenly disappear from the horse's field of vision. As well as being out of sight, we expect the horse to have his nose out in front. For some horses this is a big ask if their previous experience is limited to the comfort of following the handler's signals on the ground.

Essentially, when we ride, the horse has to learn a new language. When we are on the ground he can respond to our visual body language signals. When we ride, he has to receive direction and transition information via the reins and the rider's body tension and weight shifts.

It is easy to see how a horse with an experienced, balanced, soft-handed rider, who has taught verbal and touch signals on the ground, will get a much better deal than a novice horse struggling with a novice, unbalanced rider unfamiliar with ground work.

Some horses know a lot of riding signals but not much else because they have not been educated with ground work. Some people feel safer riding their horse than being on the ground with him.

This is sad, because both the horse and the handler are missing out on fun and the many rider-less gymnastic exercises that benefit the horse.

It's also sad because it sometimes results in riding horses that are unreliable and dangerous to handle for everyday management, through no fault of their own.

The Language of Horses

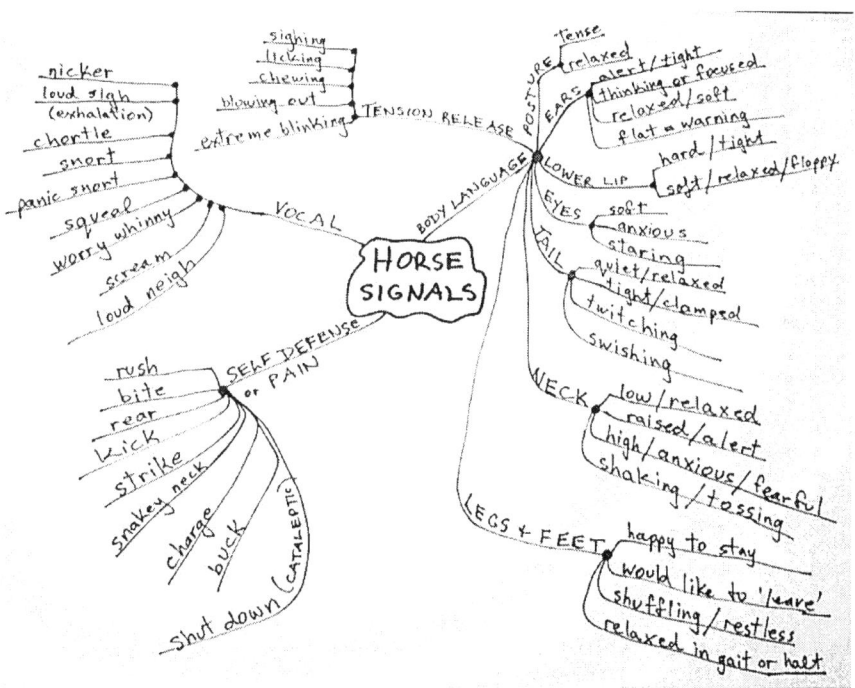

Figure 52: Horses are prey animals, so most of their communication with each other is via silent body language.

Horses have a sophisticated language designed to converse with other horses. It consists mainly of finely tuned body language and a few sounds. Horses use the same language to communicate with humans. It is up to us to learn their language so we can interpret the horse's meaning as accurately as possible. My book, *Conversations with Horses*, looks at horse signals in detail.

Horse communication is designed to cater for a social lifestyle in open areas where group members remain in visual contact. This makes body language much more important to horses than vocal communication.

The more aware we are of the signals we are giving the horse, the easier it will be to reduce the 'background static' that makes it hard for horses to read what we would like them to do.

The quieter we can be between the meaningful signals we give the horse, the easier it is for him to learn. Once we become aware of this, we can focus on keeping our body quieter between requests and keeping our voice quiet unless we are giving a voice signal.

My book, *Walking with Horses: The Eight Leading Positions* delves into the importance of how we orientate our body to the horse when we are on the ground. It includes 20 Training Plans about tasks we can teach with the various leading positions.

When we write an Individual Education Program, we have to think carefully about the signals we will use. Usually signals arise naturally out of the nature of the task. The more things we teach a horse, the more care we have to take about making each signal distinct.

Boots and I play with *target your butt to my hand* and *please move your butt away*. For teaching, I added a vocal signal to *butt away* to keep it distinct from the *target your butt to my hand* signal and the *lift your hind foot please* signal. These are the sorts of details you always have to work out between yourself and a particular horse. We can now do them all with gesture signals only.

#66 HorseGym with Boots looks at how Boots and I refined our signals so that we could communicate the three moves mentioned above, as well as a few more, carried out while I am facing the side of the horse (Leading Position 8).

Boots and I went through some confusion before we got the signals sorted. Most of the confusion arose because I had trouble being truly consistent.

What makes sense to one horse may not work at all with another horse. You have to reach a mutual agreement with the horse, and once it is reached, be sure to record exactly what your signal is. Especially if it is not one you use every day and if you have several horses. The horse is usually better at remembering than the human!

Video Clips

Video clips of people we enjoy watching are a great source of inspiration. We can pick up ideas for experimentation. We can watch in slow motion to find the nuances of what the handler and the horse are doing.

Even more enlightening is to watch clips of ourselves with our horse. It is a super way to get feedback. We can note what the horse's body language is saying – something that's hard to do when we are in the actual process of being with the horse.

We can see how clear (or not) our signals were. We can get a better idea of exactly what the horse is responding to. We can notice the background static of unnecessary movements and verbal diarrhoea that cause confusion for the horse.

If we do clicker training, we can note when the timing of our click was good and when it was less good. We can look at our treat delivery system and determine if there are ways we can improve it.

If we are using 'release reinforcement' only, how well timed are our releases?

If you are able to video some of your horse work, it really is worth the time and effort.

Horse Folder

As mentioned earlier, keeping a Horse Folder means we can easily put our hands on our:

- mind maps
- general training plans
- individual Education Program (IEP) versions
- progress logs.

As I write this book, I frequently refer to my mind maps to give me a feel for what I have covered and what topics still need work.

Reviewing the mind maps gives me a refreshing look at the central topic and the branches radiating from it. A lot of mental activity happens subconsciously behind the scenes when a subject matter is topical in our mind.

Our minds tend to work around a topic, chewing it over in the background and making new connections. Writing a book (and reading one) is a linear process, but our brain does not usually make connections in a linear way.

A 'brainwave' or a 'great idea' or 'seeing the light' is a result of our brain cells making new connections and bringing them to our conscious attention.

It's easy to underestimate the importance of keeping a written record of what we do with our horses. When we write a Training Plan or an IEP, we can let ideas flow freely, knowing that we can add, remove or alter things as we get new ideas and feedback from practice.

Since each horse and handler combination is totally unique, only the handler and horse together can create the program that best suits both of them.

The format of written records, especially the progress logs, has to be a style that suits, and not be so complex that we forget to write our notes because we run out of time. I've used a variety of formats and each has its good points and its drawbacks.

Here are examples of pen and paper Progress Logs I have used. I usually keep them in the tack room and fill them in right after a training session.

Daily Diary Format

The format shown in Figure 53 has seven days on one page. I used it to record brief summaries of daily interactions with two horses. Each horse had her own diary.

The big 'G' in the top right corner of Figure 53 tells me this was my thoroughbred, Gypsy's diary. 'Jan' at the top tells me it was January, one of our hottest months in New Zealand.

'RP' stands for round pen and it seems we were working on liberty tasks in the round pen.

I can't remember what the K3, K4, K5 and K6 mean, which is a good reminder that if we use abbreviations in our logs, we have to include a key of what they mean! There is a tidy key on the back cover of the diary, but K is not one of the entries.

'D' and 'R'ds' identify the owners of the properties we rode on.

On Tuesday, the capital E with an arrow in front of it means 'high energy'.

On Wednesday and Thursday p.m. Gypsy came along at liberty while I walked with my young horse down the farm track. On Saturday I trimmed Gypsy's front feet.

The +2% means that the exercises we did on our ride felt improved over last time.

This diary is from nine years ago. Reading it, I can still visualise the round pen, the tracks and the many paddocks we rode in.

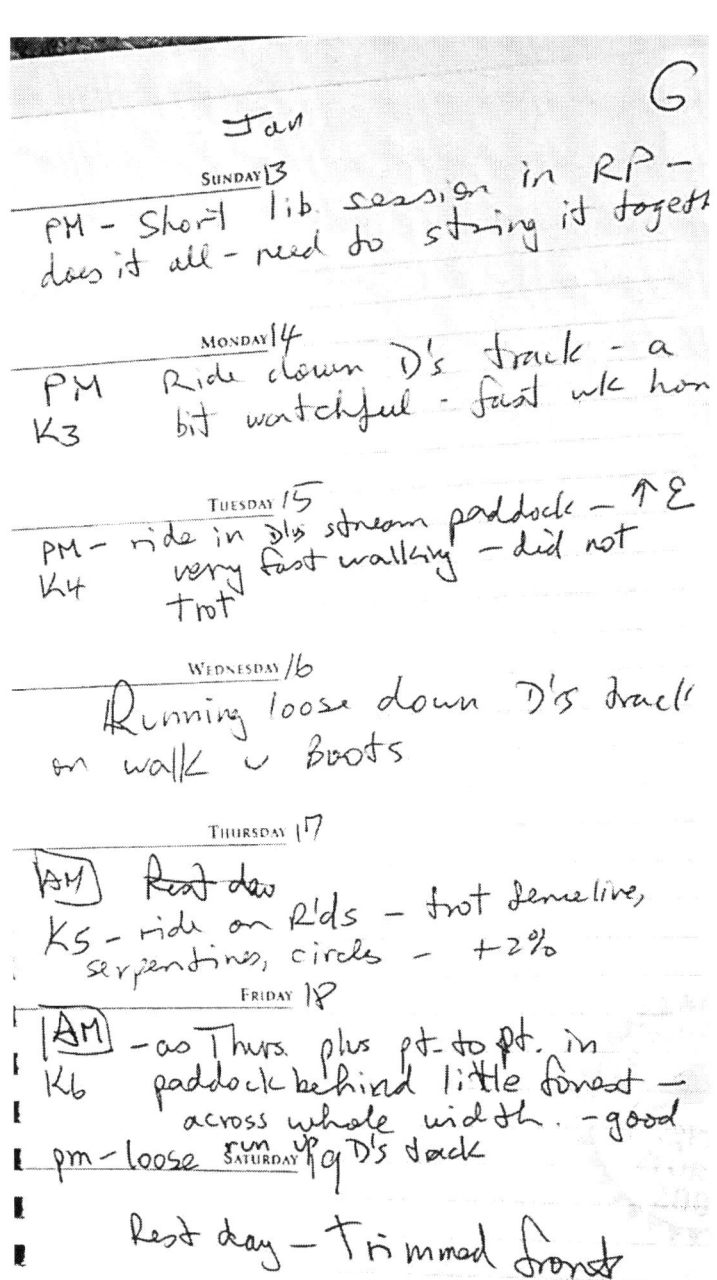

Figure 53: Horse Training Log: Diary format with a full week on one page.

Specific Task Diary

Figure 54 shows diary entries that record a specific learning sequence; in this case, building the horses' confidence with trailer loading (floating) and traveling.

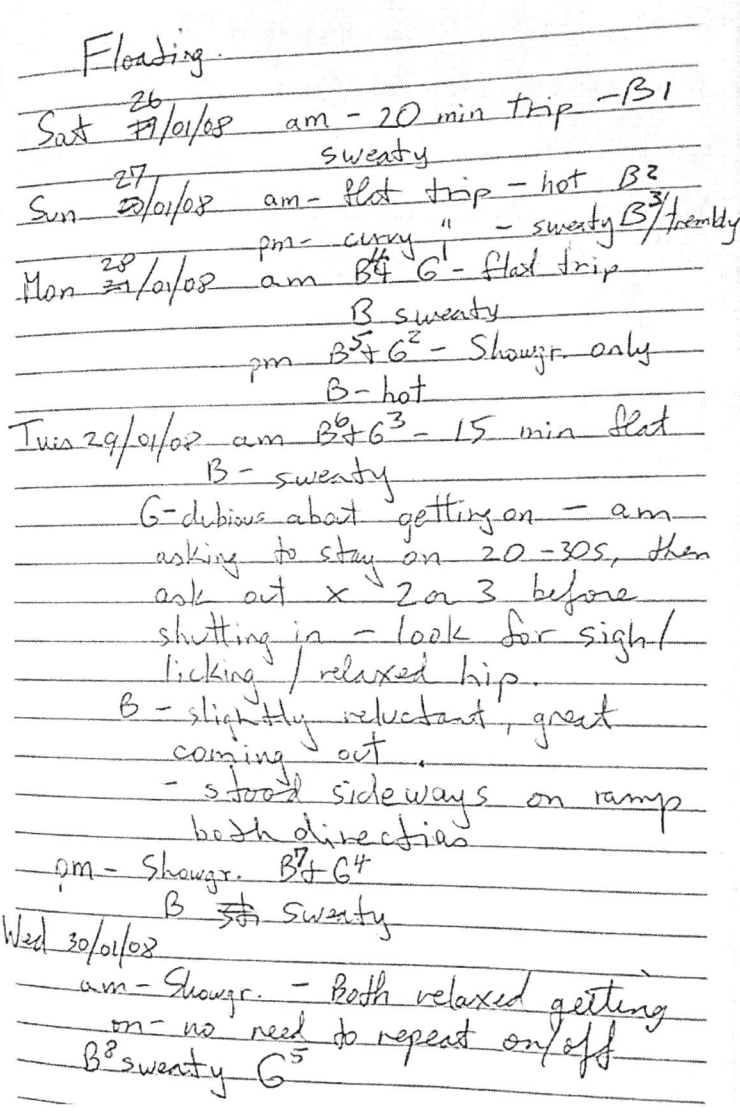

Figure 54: Training Log for building confidence with a specific task; in this case, trailer loading (floating) and traveling.

B refers to Boots and G refers to Gypsy. The number with each initial tells me how many trailer trips the horse has done in this training sequence. Boots did the first three trips by herself.

The first trips were round trips, starting and finishing at home. The last two trips were to the local showgrounds for a play and reloading to come home.

Chart Format

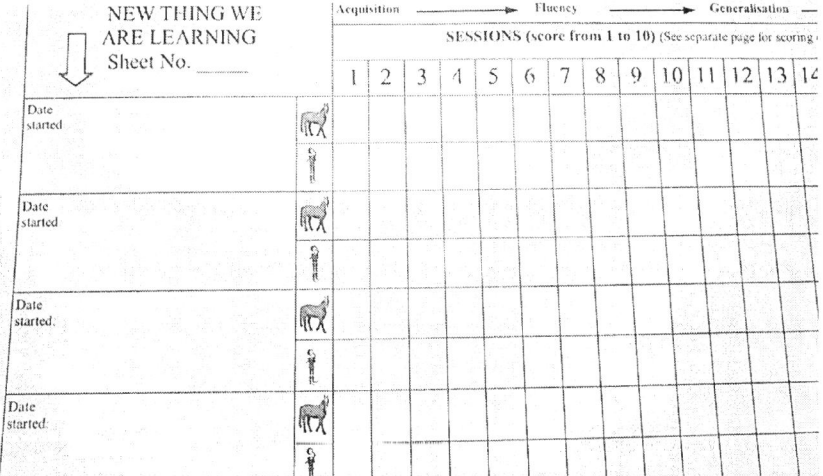

Figure 55: A chart to quickly document what we did and how well it went.

When life is busy, this type of chart makes it quick to keep track of what we did when, and how we felt each session went. The first column includes the date and states our aim or objective clearly.

If we don't want to score each session, we can simply put a tick which tells us how many days we've worked on a particular task or a slice of a particular task.

If you do want to add a value judgement to each session, you can use the space to record a score that indicates how well you think you did, and how well the horse seems to be coming along. We can score each session out of ten for both the horse and the handler. A top score of ten would be achieved:

- for the handler: when smooth, consistent, low energy signals are used
- for the horse: when the task is carried out willingly and with fluency each time it is requested.

Your scoring criteria will be personal to you, depending on the training system that you use.

Figure 56 shows a set of criteria that relate nicely to an approach where either (or both) the horse and handler are learning basic skills using release reinforcement, maybe paired with reward reinforcement.

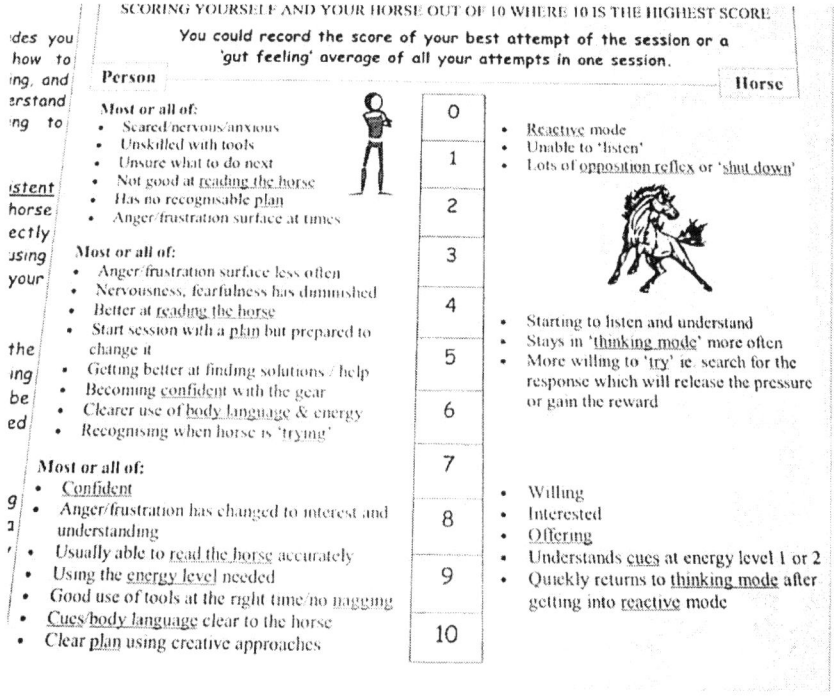

Figure 56: A possible set of scoring criteria for a horse or handler (or both) just starting out or overcoming fear issues.

Criteria such as these can be used to determine a score out of ten for a session's work on a specific task.

Figure 57 is an example of using this scoring system while I was working on (1) ridden figure eight at trot without reins and (2) teaching canter departures as groundwork.

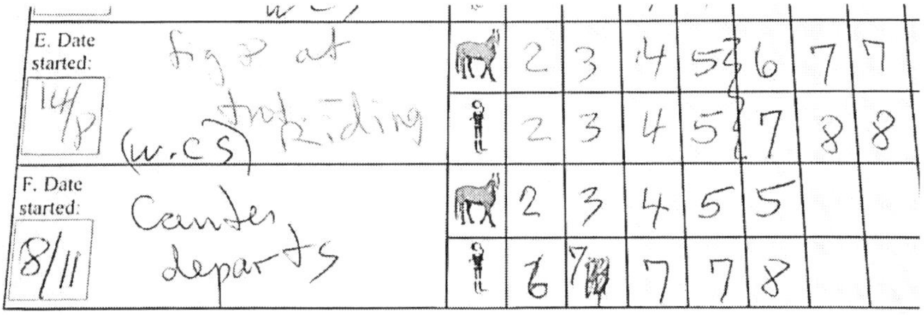

E. Date started: 14/8	fig 8 at trot riding (w.cs)	🐴	2	3	4	5 3	6	7	7
		🚶	2	3	4	5 7	7	8	8
F. Date started: 8/11	Canter departs	🐴	2	3	4	5	5		
		🚶	6	7	7	7	8		

© Hertha James, *POWERWORD PUBLICATIONS*

Figure 57: Chart that includes a 'score' out of 10 for the horse and another score out of 10 for the handler.

You can see that we were both new to trotting figure eight using weight shift and a body extension (code = w.cs) instead of reins for changing direction. Over the course of seven sessions things were starting to feel smoother. I started out pretty rubbish, but as I got better with handling the body extension, the horse magically got better too.

The squiggly line after session 4 indicates that session 5 was not the next day. Life or weather must have caused a break in continuity.

Looking at the canter departs, it seems I wasn't doing too badly. Since it was new learning for Boots, she started at 2/10 on the first day but in a couple of days she was getting the hang of it and scoring 5/10. The scores suggest that my technique had improved too.

As we develop and practice our skills, feedback from self and horse tells us:

- where to put our focus
- how to improve our communication
- how to pick the best moments for release, reward and celebration.

Since I normally work with several tasks during one session, using a chart like this allows me to quickly record how each task went while it is still fresh in my mind.

Criteria are never written in stone. The criteria we make up, for ourselves and our horse, as long as they are specific and realistic, will generally be the best ones.

If our Individual Education Program (IEP) uses clicker training (reward reinforcement) the criteria can be set out differently.

Clicker Training Logs

Example One: Willing Haltering

If we use clicker training, our chart might simply be a logical list of thin-slices. As we achieve each one, we mark it off.

If we get lost somewhere in the program, such a chart makes it easy to decide which slice we should return to, so we can remain continually successful as we work forward again.

The following chart is an example of one way to set out a Training Plan and IEP so that it's easy to document our progress. The example I've chosen is teaching a horse to willingly put his head into a halter (see Figure 58). Each numbered item in the chart is one slice of a Training Plan.

Because we are free-shaping the haltering behavior, the horse's action appears first in the chart. The handler's focus is on correctly presenting the hoop or halter, timing the clicks as accurately as possible, and delivering the treat promptly after each click.

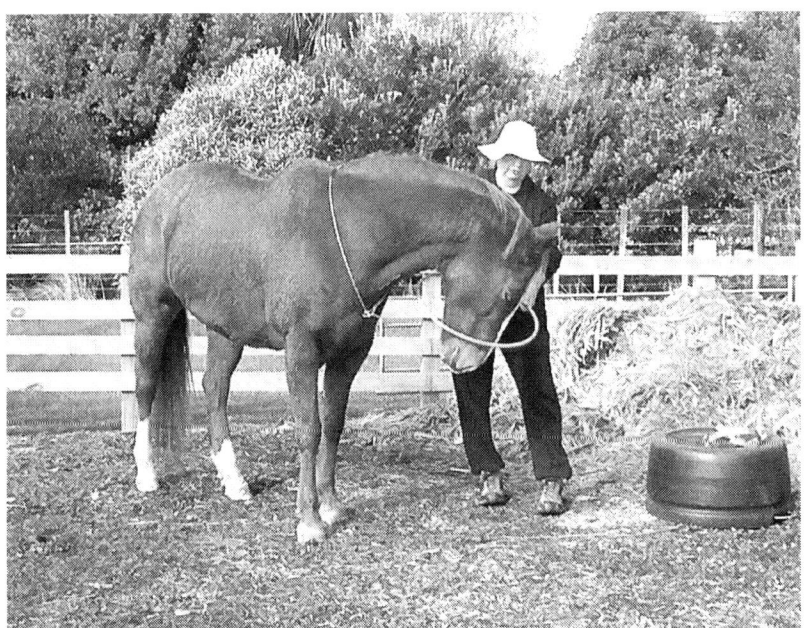

Figure 58: Teaching willing haltering; I'm free-shaping this behavior, so the horse's action is written first in the Training Plan chart that follows.

#65 HorseGym with Boots shows this process in action.

Progress Log for Teaching/Learning Willing Haltering

Slices (Criteria)	Achieved or Score
1. Horse sniffs hoop	
1. Timing of click for first sniff of hoop	
2. Horse puts nose thru hoop even a tiny bit	
2. Timing of click to capture first drop of nose toward or into hoop	
3. Horse puts a bit more of his nose thru hoop	
3. Timing of click to get a bit more nose thru hoop	

4. Horse consistently drops his nose into hoop to earn his click&treat	
4. Timing of click to keep horse continually successful	
5. Horse drops head lower when hoop is held lower	
5. Timing of click as horse lowers head further so he can still drop his nose thru hoop	
6. Horse relaxed with touch of handler's right arm across neck while his nose is in the hoop	
6. Timing of click as arm first touches neck	
7. Horse relaxed with arm lying across neck for one second while his nose is in the hoop	
7. Timing of click one second after arm is placed across neck	
8. Horse relaxed with arm lying across neck, while his nose is in the hoop, for slightly longer	
8. Timing of clicks to increase duration one second at a time to 3 seconds	
9. Horse turns head toward handler when hoop is moved left and drops his nose into the hoop	
9. Timing of click for any attempt to turn head toward hoop	
10. Horse relaxed with turning head, dropping his nose into the hoop and the handler's arm placed across his neck	
10. Timing of click with arm in place & head turned toward hoop	
11. Horse stays relaxed if hoop is pulled up as far as his eyes and removed again	
11. Timing of click as hoop passes up to eye level	

12. Horse stays relaxed if hoop is pulled up over ears & removed again	
12. Timing of click as hoop passes ears	
13. Horse relaxed when hoop is pulled up & rested behind the ears	
13. Timing of clicks for gradual duration of hoop resting behind ears	
*14. Horse retains the behavior with an *open halter instead of a hoop*	
14. Smoothly lay right arm over neck and hold halter open for horse	
15. Horse willingly turns head & drops nose into halter held open	
15. Timing of click as nose drops into halter	
16. Horse relaxed with repeats of arm over neck and halter held open	
16. Timing of click to allow nose to drop well into halter	
17. Horse relaxed with pulling up halter & laying strap behind the ears	
17. Establish as many click points as needed to build confidence with this part of the process	
18. Horse relaxed as halter is pulled on fully, then taken off again	
18. Click point is halter in position ready to be done up	
19. Horse's head relaxed toward handler while halter is done up	
19. Click upon completion of doing up halter	
20. Horse's head relaxed toward handler while halter is slipped off	

20. Timing of click as halter slips off & head is still toward handler	
21. Horse is relaxed with halter on & off several times in a row	
21. Timing of clicks for (1) completion of each haltering and (2) taking halter off	

When our slices are clearly outlined like this, it's easy to mark the slice at which we finished a session. In the next session, we can quickly run through earlier slices again to establish a relaxed, confident starting point for the new lesson.

The chart has a line for the horse's achievement and a line for the handler to make a value judgement on the timing accuracy of his or her clicks.

The better our timing with the click, the easier it is for the horse to figure out what exactly will earn his next click&treat; i.e., what it is we would like him to do.

Example Two: Free-Shaping Front Feet onto a Mat

The next chart is an example that could be used to record the progress of a horse first learning to be interested in a mat and learning to put his feet on it, using the free-shaping technique. The setting up of this task is explained after the chart.

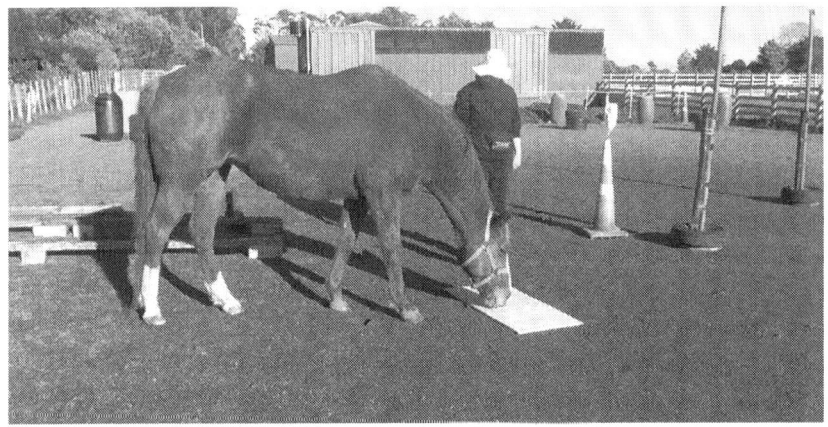

Figure 59: Free-shaping an approach to a mat. This mat is a piece of plywood. To encourage the horse's interest, I put a piece of carrot on the board while she was watching, then released her to approach the board in her own time. She is in the process of picking up the carrot strip.

Progress Chart: Free-Shaping Front Feet onto a Mat

Slices (Criteria)	Tick
1. Horse looks at mat	
1. Timing of my click (go to horse to deliver treat, then move away again)	
2. Horse moves toward mat	
2. Timing of my click at first movement toward mat	
3. Horse investigates mat with nose or feet	
3. Timing of click to first sign of curiosity	
4. Horse applies a foot to the mat each time he approaches it – may be a pawing action	
4. Timing of click for first foot touch <u>or</u> end of pawing	
5. Horse approaches the mat willingly and steps on it without pawing	
5. Timing of click after firm planting of foot	

6. Horse consistently places front feet on the mat to earn his click&treat		
6. Gradually withhold click to get more duration of feet quiet on mat		
7. Horse reliably lands both front feet on a mat and stands with feet still; self-motivated		
7. Click&treat each time the horse lands on the mat in order to establish a strong history of reinforcement		
8. Horse reliably lands both front feet on a mat and stands with feet still; on request with halter and lead		
8. Click&treat for feet placed quietly on the mat when it is requested		
9. Horse reliably lands both front feet on a mat and stands with feet still, on request at liberty		
Click&treat for feet placed quietly on the mat when it is requested		
10. Generalize: hind feet on a mat, single specific foot on a mat, all four feet on a mat, backing off a mat, backing onto a mat, different kinds of mats		

The chart has a line to record the horse's achievement, and a line to record a value judgement on the timing of the handler's click.

Free-shaping is a delightful technique that we can do with clicker-savvy horses. We observe the horse in a relaxed manner until he does something that we would like to shape into a specific behavior, e.g., placing the feet on a mat as in our example.

As soon as we notice the first hint of interest about the mat, we click&treat, going to the horse to deliver the treat. We then move away from the horse and resume observing in a relaxed manner, maybe sitting in a chair.

The mat could be a tarp laid out and pinned down, a piece of carpet, an old electric blanket, a doormat or a piece of plywood (ensure it doesn't flip up if the horse stands on one end of it).

If the horse ignores the mat, we can make it more interesting by putting a piece of carrot, apple or a bit of favorite vegetation on the mat, to pique his curiosity (Figure 59).

The horse needs to be able to see what we are doing as we set out the mat. We can have someone hold the horse, tie him up or have him behind a gate.

We click as soon as the horse interacts with the mat, then immediately go to him to deliver the treat. Next, we need a way to separate the horse and the mat so we can do it again.

We can either clip on a lead and ask the horse to move away, or we can move the mat.

If the mat is small enough, we can pick it up and toss it a distance away. Once we've tossed the mat or unclipped the lead rope (if we led the horse away from the mat), we step away and resume observing the horse in a relaxed, indirect manner. We don't want to be standing rigidly and staring at him.

Although this is free-shaping a behavior, we have obviously manipulated the environment and the object (mat) to give the horse a particular puzzle to work out.

The magic of free-shaping is that it gives the horse time and space to make up his own mind without further pressure except the desire to earn another click&treat.

Figure 60: Once the horse has taught himself about putting his feet on a mat, we can add halter and lead. To build the habit of a straight approach, I like to play with the mat between two raised rails.

We can tick each 'horse criterion line' on the chart when it is achieved. On the handler line, we could rate the timing of our clicks out of five or ten. The better the timing of our click, the faster the horse can understand exactly what we want him to do to earn his next click&treat.

How quickly a horse/handler combination progresses through a program depends on many factors that we will look at in Chapter 6.

Horse Folder – Paper and/or Digital

If we keep a digital Horse Folder as well as our pen and paper documents, regular back-up onto a memory stick or into the Cloud is probably a good idea.

Our Horse Folder will grow to contain memorabilia of all the things we are doing with our horse.

It will document the progress of our horse(s) and it will document the progress we are making with writing Training Plans and IEPs and carrying them out to achieve our objectives.

Mind maps can be reviewed and re-written as we get better ideas and make new connections. They can give us starting points for topics we want to explore further.

We can look back on Plans and IEPs we've written and change or improve them.

Once we have written our first Individual Education Program for a horse, we can look back over it with hindsight and see what we can do differently with the next one.

When we have an IEP already written for one horse, we can tweak it to take into account the character type, background, and training venues for a different horse. It makes new planning much easier and quicker than starting again from the beginning.

Chapter 5 looks at another important piece of the horse training challenge; *Understanding Pressure*.

Chapter 5

Thinking about Pressure

Pressure is not a dirty word. Everything in our life is about balancing the pressures bombarding us. The same is obviously true for horses. The pressures on domestic horses living in close and constant proximity to humans are very different from the pressures experienced by horses living in the wild.

We sometimes forget that horses are adapted to the pressures of the wild, not the pressure of the domestic situations we put them in. A mere few thousand years held captive by humans has minor impact on their genetic make-up.

People have bred horses selectively for speed, strength, size, shape, colour, way of going and a tractable nature, but the psyche of the horse remains the same as his wild ancestors and present-day wild cousins.

All the wild horses found in various places around the globe are feral horses, not truly wild like zebras. This strongly suggests that the switch from captive horse to wild horse happens fairly easily.

Done correctly, foal imprinting is helpful for captive horses because it allows a foal to view people as a natural part of his wider extended family as soon as he is born. It makes it easier for him to see people as a normal part of his life and as potential buddies.

If we enrich a foal's life with careful introduction to the events that will be part of his captive existence, there is no need for the future trauma of 'breaking in' a horse.

Horses are not adapted biologically to the pressures people put on them. Individual domestic horses have to do the best they can with the situations in which they find themselves.

People are not biologically adapted to sit for eight hours a day. Yet many modern jobs require constant sitting. Individual people, captive to the requirements of their paying jobs, have to do the best they can in the situation their workplace presents.

Reflex actions

A reflex action is an instinctive response. It is something we do (or any animal does) without thinking about it first. A reflex action can be to move away, like jerking our hand away when it touches something hot. Maybe our whole body jumps away when we see a cockroach in our sock drawer.

I once found a wild rat in my sock drawer. My reflex action was memorable, even though I've often kept rats as pets.

A reflex action can also be to move toward something, like grabbing a child about to run onto the road. Or rapidly shifting our foot to the brakes when the brake lights of the car in front come on, or a cat dashes across the road.

Generally, reflex actions are concerned with physical safety. One good jolt from an electric fence can modify our behavior around electric fences for a long time.

Horses, being prey animals, rely on flight for safety and have a strong set of instinctive responses. We need to be aware of these and recognize them for what they are: the natural reflex actions of a prey animal.

When a horse reacts against pressure that he doesn't understand, our actions have put him into survival mode. He is not being bad, stubborn, stupid or any of the other value-judgements that people love to make.

If the horse reads the human as something to fear, his instinctive response is to move away. When we contain him with ropes and fences, he can't follow his first instinct to flee. The only options left for him are to bite, strike, kick and rear as he would when he is confronted by predators.

By carefully teaching a horse the responses that we want, we can replace the horse's natural instinctive reflexes with the taught responses. A well-educated horse will offer the learned alternatives unless he feels himself in danger.

In other words, we need to put in the time, patience and effort that allow the horse to understand the situations in which he finds himself as a domestic horse. This is what training is all about. We have to give the horse opportunities to decide for himself that the humans in his life are not a danger.

We also have to help the horse discover that it is possible to understand the meanings behind human touch, gesture and voice.

Horse trainers often refer to instinctive reflex actions as 'opposition reflexes', no doubt because the horse is 'opposing' the pressure the person is putting on him. Obviously, if we pull on a horse's head with a rope, he will instinctively pull back if we have not carefully taught him that pressure behind his ears can be relieved by moving forward.

In times of stress, horses instinctively move toward the middle of their herd, since the middle is the safest place. If we are the other member of the horse's herd during a scare, his reflex action will be to move in toward us. He will expect us to be as robust as another horse, so this can be problematic.

If a horse does something that results in a food reward he enjoys, his instinctive reflex will be to repeat that movement (or stillness) to see if the reward is forthcoming again. In other words, repeating a rewarded action is just as strong a reflex as avoiding an action that has an unpleasant consequence.

Daily survival by all people and other animals is a balance between seeking more of what we like or need, and trying to avoid what we dislike or fear.

Horses instinctively move away from anything coming toward them, and toward anything moving away. These are all useful things to know as we strive to give our horses confidence in different situations and different venues, keeping ourselves safe while we do it.

General Life Pressures Facing Horses

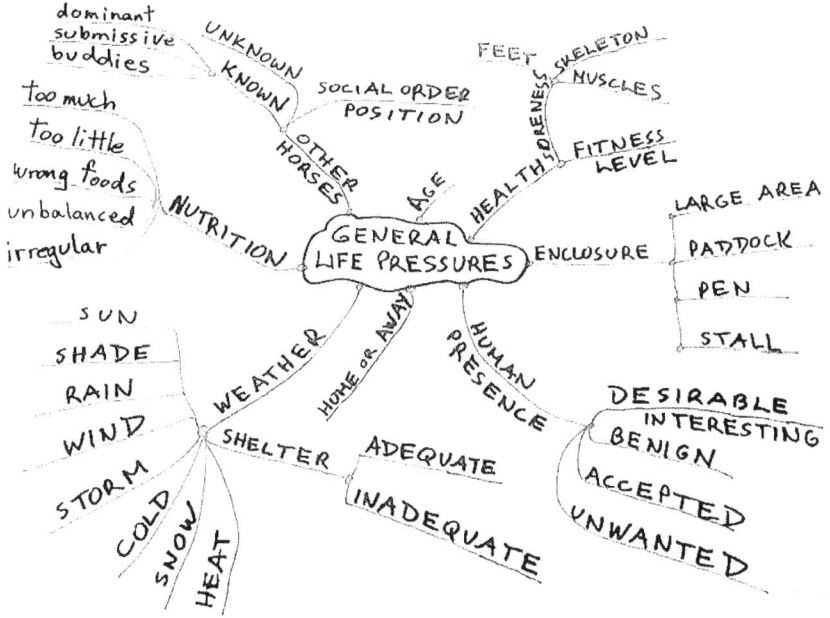

Figure 61: Some of the general life pressures faced by horses in captivity.

If we look at the 'enclosure' branch of the mind map, we note that unusual pressure on the horse increases as we go from *large area* to *stall*. Keeping an animal, whose whole biology revolves around movement, in a tiny container is not keeping him with his best interests at heart.

It may be convenient for the human, but it is cruel for the horse. So-called 'stable vices' are not vices at all. They are psychological illnesses brought about when the biological needs of horses are not met. Biological needs have physical, mental and emotional aspects.

If we approach our horse and find that his behavior suggests our presence is unwanted, we need to look to ourselves, since the horse is speaking to us very clearly. He is expressing his thoughts and feelings honestly. The only way we can cause him to feel better about his situation is to change what we do.

Thinking about the 'weather' branch of the mind map, we can see that it's important to factor in that the horse may be tired after a night of lightning, thunder and gale winds, or days of incredible heat. Do we provide shade during all parts of the day? Do we make sure the horse can get out and about in the winter sun? Are there places for all the horses to shelter out of wind from various directions?

Around Calgary, Canada, where I grew up in the 1960s, we never saw horses wearing covers. Most of them were out 24/7. Winter temperatures were often 20 or 30 degrees Fahrenheit below zero. Horses are adapted for dry cold.

The New Zealand climate has times of persistent heavy rain that wets a horse right to the skin. If it's also cold and/or windy, a cover for the duration of the wet weather avoids extreme shiver responses and possible respiratory infection. My horse, Boots, has a walk-in shelter but she only uses it when it's very hot, or cold and wet for a long time.

My winter horse wears a coat of mud prepared by herself. With regular rain, her outer longer hairs arrange themselves into little channels that funnel off the water as it falls.

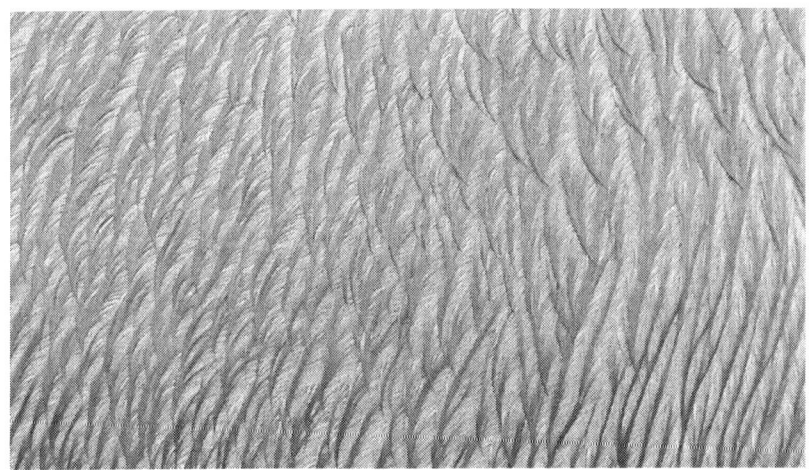

Figure 62: Unless it rains so hard that water is driven forcefully into the skin, horses with a natural winter coat prepare their own 'rainwear'.

Feeding an individual horse the correct amount of the right fodder is a continual challenge. Easy keepers get overweight and the trick is to feed a little often to keep their gut bacteria happy.

Spring and autumn grass flush causes problems with too much sugar in the fresh grass. In places like New Zealand, grass ideal for horses is not what is usually growing on farms that cater to dairy cows or rapid weight gain in sheep.

It's natural for horses to gain weight in summer and lose weight over winter, but too much new-growth spring/autumn grass without counterbalancing exercise means we have to manipulate our horse's food intake to avoid obesity and diseases like laminitis. The idea is not to withhold food, but to provide low energy long-stem roughage continuously or as frequently as possible over 24 hours.

If we keep several horses, it's nice to have them live as a group, but what if they have very different nutritional requirements?

The soil in many places is deficient in specific essential minerals such as selenium or copper. Some people forget to give their horses a salt or mineral block, which means the horses' health is probably not optimal.

If we ride, drive in harness, or ask for complex agility work, have we conditioned and coached the horse to gradually build his athletic fitness and gymnastic ability? If the horse seems unusually slow or lethargic or uninterested, do we check out his teeth, his feet, his skeletal alignment and look out for possible sore muscles?

Do we understand the pressures we put on a young horse if we ride or train hard before the joints mature? When we retire a horse, do we make sure he has plenty of natural movement and interactions to keep him mentally and emotionally active?

Do we understand the pressures that arise between horses in captivity? When we introduce a new horse to an established group, can we do it across a safe fence? Is the paddock big enough so that the new horse can easily get away from every one of the other horses? Do we make sure there are no places where the new horse can be trapped?

Human Pressures

Beyond these general pressures, let's take a closer look at the other types of pressures that face domestic horses.

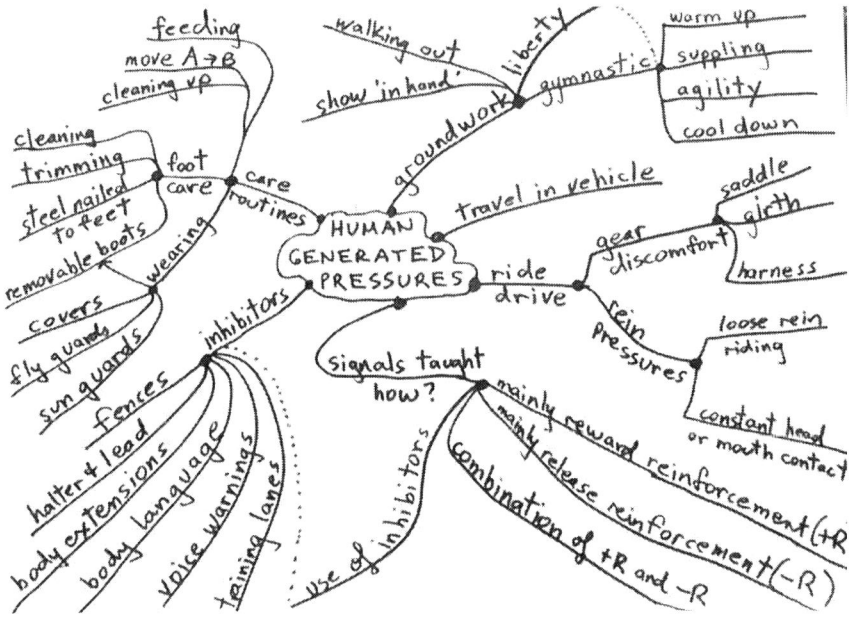

Figure 63: Human Generated Pressures

A horse that hasn't been taught to respond to human actions in a way that allows people to feel safe around him is a horse without the resilience to live a calm, full life in captivity.

When I was a zookeeper and wild animal handler on film sets in the 1970s, a book called *The Management of Wild Animals in Captivity* by Lee S. Crandall was the handiest of resources. This was long before the days of the Internet.

Working with many different species in captivity made me highly conscious that when we keep horses, we have removed them from their natural life in family groupings. They are a 'wild animal in captivity'.

The management of horses in captivity is a theme of many books. However, rather than beginning with natural horse behaviour, most books look at domestic horses from the viewpoint of problems to be solved. The so-called problems that horses have in captivity are a result of human actions.

People expect horses to do things that no wild horse would ever be faced with. We ask (force) horses to do things that zookeepers wouldn't dream to ask of the animals in their care.

The era of *Chimps' Tea Parties* is thankfully over in most places.

Figure 64: My husband, Bryan, was the last zookeeper at Wellington Zoo, N.Z. to be asked to put on Chimps' Tea Parties. *Zoos now try to keep social animals like chimps living in family groupings in large enclosures rather than make them into parodies of humans. Soft drinks and riding in trucks are probably off the menu too!*

Horses are not quite so fortunate. Their lives in captivity are often either incredibly dull or they are made to carry out physical tasks for which they are not adapted.

Horses are not anatomically structured to carry weight, jump great heights repeatedly or move in continuous circles. They don't have the spinal flexibility that allows cats (and dogs to a lesser extent) to bend and jump easily.

Horses are not physiologically designed to stand endless hours isolated in stalls or to be fed 'meals'. Their circulatory system depends on 24/7 whole-body movement so that blood from the feet is pushed up the long legs back to the heart. Activity is punctuated by frequent short rests. Their digestive system requires a steady inflow of low calorie, long-stemmed forage.

More and more horse owners are trying hard to allow their horses to live with 24-hour freedom of movement and contact with other horses. Authors like Jaime Jackson have given us the idea of the 'paddock paradise' where the horses' living area is set up to encourage maximum movement and adequate forage across 24 hours. Details about Jaime's book are in the Reference List.

More people are recognizing that their horse is a wild animal in captivity. More people are learning to use *reward reinforcement* in the form of clicker training, along with traditional *release reinforcement* to teach the horse the skills that he needs to get along with people in various contexts.

Most horses are still controlled by applying pressure to the most sensitive parts of their anatomy: the inside of their mouth, pressure on their chin groove and behind their ears. Pressure in these areas easily becomes painful.

The greatest thing that Pat Parelli did for millions of horses is to get their riders out of their mouths, at least until the rider has a relatively stable seat on the horse and does not use the reins as a means of holding on to maintain balance.

Since the popularization of Parelli Natural Horsemanship, many people have learned to ride bridle-less and many more have learned to use a rope hackamore or bridle with finesse, and to avoid contact on the horse's mouth or head unless they want to give a signal.

Most horses manage to put up with the pressures people put on them because most horses are quick learners and because they have no choice. They are captive to a foreign species.

Horses that don't conform to the straightjackets into which people put them are passed on and often end up in a situation of neglect or in a tin. The stress and trauma many horses go through before ending up ignored in a field or fed to a dog are concerns for a growing number of people.

As mentioned earlier, there are lots of books written about horses and how to manage them or train them for specific disciplines in what people refer to as sport ('sport' from the human viewpoint).

There are a few books and blogs (and some video footage) that attempt to describe natural horse behavior in the wild. If people would access these before bringing a horse into their life, horses might get a better deal.

A person armed with information about natural horse behavior would probably develop a more empathetic outlook toward the horses in their care.

If we understand more fully how horses survive in the wild, we can more easily see the bizarre nature of the things we expect this blameless animal to do. And how unnaturally people often expect horses to live.

High Level Awareness

It's been said that lack of confidence is a horse's default setting. But I would hazard a guess that this observation was made with horses in situations where they are expected to do un-horse-like things.

Horses are genetically wired to have a high level of awareness. Much of what people want to do with horses requires shutting down most of this high level of awareness and forcing the horse to instead pay attention to learning ways of minimizing pain in the mouth or aggressive whip/spur actions.

In the more benign training systems, horses are taught how to respond to horse-like body language on the ground, and given time and opportunity to learn new signals, without mouth trauma, when their person mounts up.

When we do ground work with horses, it's easy to see and appreciate just how astute horses are, and how sensitive they are to body language despite the strong accent we must have.

These ideas are explored and developed in my other books:
- *Conversations with Horses: An in-depth look at the Signals and Cues between Horses and their Handlers*
- *Walking with Horses: The Eight Leading Positions*
- *Learning Universal Horse Language: No Rope Necessary*

When we ride, most of our body language becomes invisible to the horse. When we work or play with the horse on the ground, it's a much more even playing field for the horse.

It's not hard for people to learn Universal Horse Language to communicate easily with a horse at liberty. We can observe the responses of the horse's whole body, his neck, eyes, ears, tail and lower lip.

A solid foundation of ground work establishes a two-way communication system. Quite a few signals can be taught on the ground and easily transfer to riding; for example:

- tap behind withers for 'walk on' (touch pressure)
- hand on neck for 'head down' (touch pressure)
- breath in for 'energy up' (energy up communication)
- breath out for 'energy down' (energy down communication)
- touch at girth for stepping sideways (touch pressure)
- touch on shoulder to yield the forequarters (touch pressure)
- touch near hip to yield the hindquarters (touch pressure)
- halter touch on the side of the head for turning right and left (touch pressure)
- voice 'walk on' signal (learned behavior pressure)
- voice 'back' signal (learned behavior pressure)
- voice 'whoa' signal (learned behavior pressure)

- voice 'trot' and 'canter' signals (learned behavior pressure).

It's easy to see that when we ride, we can keep using the breathing and touch pressure signals. For the forequarter and hindquarter yields, we can teach the horse that the touch will come from our leg moving forward or back from the girth by replacing the hand signal with a similar leg signal.

We use the new signal (leg position), followed by the old signal either carried out by a person on the ground or by using a body extension for the new touch signal. The horse will soon respond to the new riding signal and we can phase out the ground-work signal.

I've defined voice signals as *learned behavior pressure* because when a horse understands something well, he usually responds promptly and willingly.

Another example of *learned behavior pressure* is when we use the keenness of a horse to touch a nose target to 'draw' him into stepping forwards, backwards, sideways to reach the target.

If touching the nose to a target is highly reinforced with click&treat, presenting the nose target is a form of pressure in the same way as a touch to ask for a yield is pressure.

Likewise, if we have taught voice signals with a long history of consistency and reinforcement, using them applies the pressure of a learned behavior.

It doesn't matter whether the horse learned the behavior with reward reinforcement, release reinforcement, or a combination of both.

Figure 65: Boots is following a target on the end of a stick that I'm using to 'draw' her through the S-bend, which is a favorite Horse Agility obstacle. I'm also using the voice signal, "Around", to indicate the U-turn she has to make to stay inside the S-bend, rather than walk forward over the rail in front of her. Her willingness to follow the target is an example of what I've called 'learned behavior pressure'.

We can also teach a voice "Whoa" signal by timing the word to the moment a horse intends to stop anyway as he reaches a nose target, a mat or a pile of hay.

Once a horse understands a voice signal, the signal given carries with it the pressure of an expectation to be fulfilled. We could call it a habit. The horse has formed the habit of halting when we say, "Whoa". Many horses have formed the habit of moving up a gait when their handler gives a clucking or smooching voice signal.

'Walk on', 'Halt', 'Back Up' 'Trot' and 'Canter' voice signals can be taught by having the horse shadow our body energy and movement on the ground. Then the signals can be generalized to use when we are riding or the horse is moving around us, as in lunging.

Touch pressure is a natural form of communication for horses. Usually they move away from touch pressure by another horse. In some cases, their instinct is to move into the pressure, for example, the urge to move into the center of the herd in times of perceived danger. Foals press into their mother's side at times of danger.

A training example of moving into touch pressure is when we teach a horse to target our hand with various body parts. Boots loves the game of targeting her chin, ear, nose, forehead, knee, shoulder, ribs and hindquarters to my hand. Some of these are on video in *#66 HorseGym with Boots*.

Often when we begin to teach a horse to yield his hindquarters with a touch on the hip, the horse's first inclination is to move into the pressure, as he would to send a message to a subordinate herd member or a predator by lining up his hind end in preparation for a kick.

A subordinate horse will move away if he is being nudged or nipped on the butt by a higher-ranking horse. Horses higher in the social order generally move subordinate herd members with as little energy as possible. Often it is an ear flick, a grumpy look, a neck gesture, a swishing tail or a raised hind leg.

A handler using Universal Horse Language can emulate these gestures with body language and body extensions in a way that makes it easy for the horse to understand the handler's meaning. Consistency is the key. More than anything else, horses appreciate clarity from us. There is seldom a need to touch a horse in a punitive way. Strong intent and body language backed up with gestures are usually more than enough.

We also have to understand that putting a halter on a horse, which puts pressure behind the ears, activates a basic panic response. This is because predators hone in on that area to make their kill.

We can tap into the horse's *high level of awareness* in order to teach him, in a constructive way, the signals he needs to know during his life with people. If we use reward reinforcement as well as release reinforcement, horses learn very quickly. The behavior of all animals is shaped by doing more of what brings reward, and doing less of what causes discomfort.

As long as we are fair, clear and consistent, horses willingly respond to our requests if they can understand what we want. It is their high level of awareness, as well as their social nature, that makes them so trainable.

Many people have great fun interacting with their horses, ponies, donkeys and mules on the ground with no intention of ever riding.

Figure 66: Playing at liberty is a fun and rewarding way to interact with our horse if we choose not to ride or if we have ponies and small donkeys.

In my opinion, lack of confidence is not a horse's default setting unless we have placed him in a situation that has drained his confidence.

How We Add and Remove Pressure

We put pressure on our horse when we:

- look at him
- approach him

- face him front on
- touch him with our hand or body extension
- make ourselves larger
- breathe in
- raise our body energy
- show up with treats to use for reward reinforcement (clicker training)
- gesture with our hand or body extension
- put on a halter and lead
- put touch pressure on the halter via the lead rope
- give unclear signals
- use inconsistent signals
- ask something that is beyond the horse's physical, mental or emotional ability at that time
- put the horse into an unusual situation
- rush things - go too fast with new learning
- are fearful - horses sense fear pheromones easily
- are sneaky - predators are sneaky so horses are highly attuned to sneakiness
- lose our 'cool' - the horse can only be as calm and cool as we are
- correct too much, which makes the horse unwilling to try again
- change routines suddenly.

We take pressure off our horse when we:
- look away
- turn away
- move away
- shrink our size
- relax our body energy
- take up neutral body language and body extension positions
- use clear, consistent signals

- stay emotionally neutral or even better, are laughing having fun - horses easily pick up happy vibrations
- keep a 'smile' or drape in the lead rope or reins when not giving a signal
- spend dwell time together to pause during a teaching/learning session
- spend 'down time' together where all we do is hang out
- use reward reinforcement (clicker training) correctly
- recognize thresholds and retreat to where both we and the horse can find relaxation
- recognize when we need to deal with our own thresholds first
- pause and set up a task again, rather than correct a mistake
- honour the routines we've set up
- rubbing and massage – some horses enjoy this, others don't and will see it as more pressure.

As we become more aware of what we are doing and how we are doing it, we gradually learn to quickly adjust our behavior, so giving the horse the best deal possible.

Pressure Expands Our Comfort Zones

Good training begins from a place of confidence and proceeds in slices thin enough to maintain confidence most of the time. We have to become aware of when a horse is at the limit of his present comfort zone. Chapter 1 looked at comfort zones in detail.

To be a good teacher and coach for our horse, we have to think about how we can expand his comfort zone (over a variety of contexts) in a way that leaves his confidence intact.

The only way to expand the horse's comfort zone (and ours) is to apply pressure of some kind. When we take the horse beyond his comfort zone, it helps if we can stay in our own comfort zone.

When we apply the pressure of new teaching, it is ideal to have the horse in an area where he feels safe and is able to relax. If he has buddies, it helps if he can see them but they are not able to interfere with the training process.

For this purpose, a buddy pen that overlooks the training area is valuable. A safe spot to tie up a second horse is another possibility. A horse tied up with one rope can get into all sorts of difficulties, so we need to be constantly aware.

The art of thin-slicing gives us a tool that allows us to use pressure in tiny amounts. It allows learning without raising anxiety (the horse's and ours) to a level that harms the learning process.

Expressed in another way, thin-slicing allows us to nudge the horse across the edge of his comfort zone in small increments that don't arouse his anxiety to the point that he is unable to learn thoughtfully. When a horse is at the edge of his comfort zone, we say that he is 'at threshold'.

When his body language tells us that he is at threshold (higher head, increased whole body tension), we have to decide whether we can ask a bit more, or should we pause, slow down and consolidate before moving on.

Each time we nudge the threshold a little bit further, the horse has expanded his comfort zone.

The rest of the book looks at writing Training Plans and Individual Education Programs that enable us to teach new behaviors in a way that smoothly leads the handler and the horse from what they can already do together, toward the accomplishment of a new task.

Chapter 6 tackles the vexed topic of goals and objectives.

Chapter 6

Planning: Setting Goals and Objectives

The opposite of having a plan is aimlessness and procrastination. A plan gives us focus. No focus = inaction.

Author Cal Newport says, "Complex planning is a subtle skill: it requires you to both conceive of future steps and evaluate whether these steps are a good idea."

He goes on to say, "Procrastination, in my experience, is not a character flaw, but instead evidence that you don't have a believable plan for succeeding at what you're trying to do."

I would like to change the statement above to: "You don't *yet* have a clear, achievable plan for what you would like to do".

Callie Rae King gives these examples of how procrastination related to horsemanship might show itself.

- "You skip going to the barn or paddock because you don't know what to do when you get there.
- You walk out in the field and pet your horse but you don't bring him in. Why bother? Every time you ride you just do aimless circles anyway.
- You cancel your lesson because it's been a busy week - you don't have the energy for it right now."

There are links to the work of Cal Newport and Callie King in the Reference List.

To give our training direction, we have to put a certain amount of energy into planning what we want to do.

On the other hand, we can get bogged down with 'analysis paralysis', which is another type of procrastination.

We might view endless video clips of other people doing things with their horses, but find it hard to evaluate our own situation and get out there to work on our own progress.

It helps if we accept two things.
1. Learning is a messy business.
2. Teaching or coaching our horse is a form of on-going education for us.

Whenever we are teaching the horse a new task or practicing something we already know, we are learning a variety of things.
a) How well or badly are we communicating our intent to the horse today?
b) How is the horse responding to our signals today?
c) Are our responses to the horse's responses staying emotionally neutral or cheerful, or are we getting frustrated?
d) What further details about the nature of the task are coming to light?
e) How can I make learning this easier for the horse?

For example, a Horse Agility task requires the horse to lower his nose to an object about twelve inches off the ground, and keep it there for the count of two, five or ten, depending on the level of the class.

This task requires a plan that teaches a signal for the horse to lower his head. But how will he know to keep his nose on the object for a certain time? It makes sense that we need to also teach a signal for, "Head-up please".

Once head-down and head-up signals are clearly understood, we gradually lengthen the time before we give the head-up signal. If the horse is clicker-savvy, this won't take long.

If we don't use clicker training, we may have to devise a head-down signal that remains on until we ask for head-up.

An Individual Education Program (IEP) for a specific horse is always a work in progress. Each session brings new feedback that can be incorporated into the program in readiness for the next session. While the horse is learning, we are learning.

The Nitty-Gritty of Planning

The end point of every plan is a goal. Once the desired goal is clear in our mind, it's much easier to set up the steps or slices of the process that will allow us to reach our goal. We can work backwards from the goal and/or forward from the starting point. It usually takes a bit of experimentation to determine the starting point for a particular horse.

Difference between Training Plans and Individual Education Programs (IEPs)

The next two chapters look in detail at the process of creating Training Plans which can be expanded into IEPs. A Training Plan is more general than an IEP. It starts with a goal behavior and thin-slices the goal into the smallest teachable bits (slices) that the handler can think of.

The slices are then arranged into an order that makes sense to the handler and will hopefully make sense to most horses. Such a plan can be shared with other people who can adapt it to their own situation.

An Individual Education Program takes the Training Plan and amplifies it to include a particular horse's character type, age, health, fitness and previous training, as well as the relationship the horse has with the handler who is writing and carrying out the IEP.

Only the horse's handler can create an IEP because the handler's training approach, character type, energy, fitness, time management, methods of reinforcement, inhibiting strategies and knowledge of the horse's background, will all be a part of what actually takes place.

These factors are unique to each horse and handler partnership, so they can't be shared or transferred.

When we watch someone work with a horse, we can formulate a Training Plan from what we see and hear, but to have that Training Plan work for us requires knowledge about our horse and ourselves that only we can apply to the task.

Features of Useful Plans

The mnemonic *IMPROVE IT* makes a handy mental handle when we tackle a planning session.

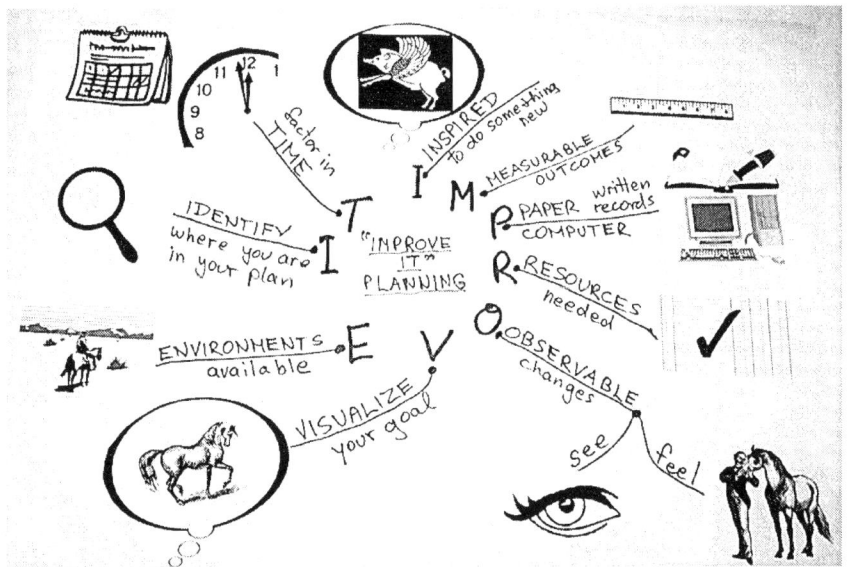

Figure 67: Nine features of useful plans can be linked to the mnemonic IMPROVE IT.

Let's look at each of the nine features in turn.

1. Inspired: Something has inspired you to buy or lease or look after a horse. Something has inspired you to form a relationship with a horse and spend time in his company. Something has inspired you to teach your horse a new skill, a new trick, or to improve something you already do.

It can be a task as basic as teaching the horse to lead politely with his neck beside your shoulder, halt when you halt and walk on when you walk on.

Or it can be as complex as teaching a horse to load himself into a trailer while you stay at the ramp.

2. Measurable: How will you know you've reached your goal? How clear and consistent will your signals be? Exactly what behaviors, and to what degree of perfection, will the horse carry out the task when the goal is achieved?

3. Paper: Your Horse Folder will fill up with your notes, diagrams, charts, mind maps, checklists, diaries and logs. It will contain Training Plans that give an overview of the possible slices that make up a specific task and Individual Education Programs (IEPs) you've written for specific horses.

As already mentioned, IEPs are expanded Training Plans. They factor in the age, health, character type and previous experiences of the horse and the handler, creating a custom-made program. IEPs must also include realistic time frames.

4. Resources: Take an inventory of what you have already in terms of gear, venues, helpers, obstacles and objects to help with the task you have decided to work with. Make a list of things you still need to organize. Keep your checklists to use again.

5. Observable Changes: As the handler and horse become tuned in to each other, the horse will take meaning from the consistent actions of the handler. At the same time, the handler will become increasingly able to see and feel more subtle changes in the horse's energy, body tension/relaxation and responses.

A good plan sets out the observable changes we will actively look for. This is done by thin-slicing the task, a skill we'll shortly investigate in more detail.

6. Visualize: How will it look and feel when you have achieved the goal? Here are a few examples of visualization.
   a. Think about walking with your horse at liberty and see him staying in step beside your shoulder.
   b. Think of directing your focus toward your horse's hindquarters and watch them move away.
   c. Think about standing at the tailgate of your trailer. See yourself giving a hand gesture as you toss the lead rope over the horse's back and he walks straight into the trailer. Maybe your vision has the horse going into the trailer at liberty.

d. Think of laying your hand gently behind the horse's ears and his head will drop down.
   e. Think of how you will organize your body in the saddle to give the signal for a canter depart and feel the horse lift himself into the canter.
   f. In your mind, lay out the ten obstacles of a Horse Agility course, and visualize your clear signals and the horse's perfect responses as you navigate each obstacle and set up for the next one.

If you ever have a problem getting to sleep, I've found that visualizing working through ten obstacles like this is more effective than counting sheep. We rarely make it past the fifth obstacle before I'm sound asleep.

7. Environment: What areas do you have available?
   a. Would a quiet, private work area be best for teaching a certain new task?
   b. Where can you train so that the horse remains confident?
   c. Do you have an area from which the horse can see his buddies but they are not able to interfere?
   d. Do you want a helper for part of the process?
   e. As the horse gains confidence, do you want more distractions?
   f. What props will you use to begin teaching a new task?
   g. When will you gradually remove the props?

8. Identify: Milestones in your plan make it easy to know exactly where you are on the route to your goal. When we use the thin-slicing process where each slice has its own behavioral objective (we'll look at these shortly), completion of each slice of the task is a mini-milestone.

If you keep a record of where you finished a session, it's easier to begin the next training session. Such records are especially helpful when life or weather cause long gaps between sessions.

9. Time: Factor in the time it will take to experiment gently with a horse to find the best starting point for his Individual

Education Program. How long do you anticipate it may take a particular horse to work through the thin-sliced program? The background and ability of the handler and the horse, plus how often you can get together, will determine the timeline.

Sometimes it will all come together much more quickly than you expected. Other times you will realize that a few prerequisites are missing and need to be added to the program. Certain things will be more difficult for some horses and some people.

If we carefully take the time it takes to gradually build the horse's (and our) confidence and skills, the new learning will eventually become old hat and a secure part of the repertoire. Then it's time to cast about for a new challenge.

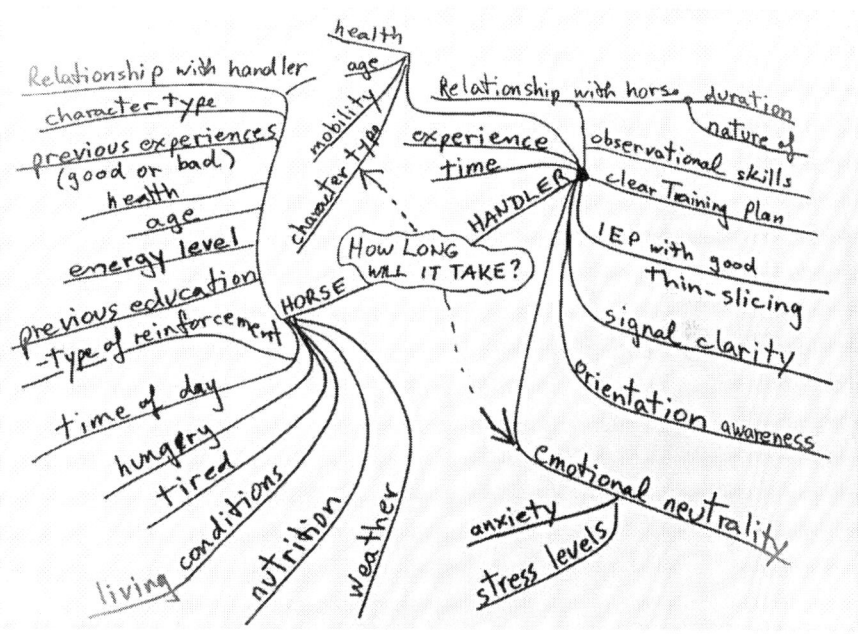

Figure 68: Some of the factors that influence how long it takes to teach a new task.

The nine features of good plans will be echoed when we look at writing the behavioral objectives that make up the slices of a plan.

Visualizing a Whole Plan

Here is a way of visualizing a whole plan. Imagine you and your horse are at the base of a mountain range. Your plan is to walk to a ranch on the far side of the mountains. Your horse (or donkey or mule) is carrying a pack with your camping essentials.

You know the details of the route and you have an idea about where you hope to spend each night of the journey. Each day is made up of tasks that lead toward your daily goal – your campsite. Each campsite is one milestone on the map of your route.

Some days you will reach your designated campsite. Other days lameness, fatigue or weather force you to change the timing element of your plan. Or you may reach a beautiful spot and decide to stay there for several days. The plan you are using to reach the ranch is flexible.

As each day progresses, you adjust the plan in response to what is actually happening. You may be familiar with the saying accredited to John Lennon, "Life is what happens when we are busy making other plans."

In the visualization of walking across the mountains with your horses, it's easy to know when you have reached each goal - your campsite for the night. It may have been a long day with arduous tasks along the way, or it may have been a warm, pleasant, short journey.

The tasks leading to each goal would be things like eating, breaking and setting up camp, caring for your horse, walking hills, crossing streams, meeting wildlife. The details of how you handle each task become the slices of that task.

Thin-Slicing

Parts of this section are from my book: *Walking with Horses: The Eight Leading Positions.*

Thin-slicing is a shorthand way of saying: split the overall task we want the horse to learn into its smallest teachable parts and teach each part in a way that makes it as easy as possible for the horse to understand.

As each tiny part of the task becomes ho-hum for the horse, move on to the next part. Gradually all the parts will come together so the overall task is seamlessly carried out with confidence and willingness.

It means starting with the most fundamental lessons and gradually adding complexity until we have shaped the whole behavior we want.

As each small part, called a slice, is mastered, we begin to teach the next slice, either separately or as a continuation of the first slice. If taught separately, once the second slice is learned, we link it to the first one.

Proceeding like this, we gradually chain all the slices together until the horse can do the whole task as a continuous movement.

We reinforce what we want by release of our signal pressure. If we do clicker training, we have a double reinforcement: first the release that accompanies the click and then the treat or payment for effort. We could call it click&pay rather than click&treat.

In this book, I refer to moments we want to reinforce as *release (click&treat)*. If you use only release reinforcement, ignore the click&treat option and replace it with what you prefer to do.

Release reinforcement means taking pressure away from the horse. It includes:
- removing signal pressure
- breathing out
- dropping our focus and body energy into relaxation
- turning away
- moving away from the horse.

Some horses enjoy scratching as a relaxation signal. Other horses aren't as keen to be touched and prefer space instead.

Although horses learn quickly with well-executed pressure and release of pressure, 'negative' or 'release reinforcement' will never provide the motivation presented by a chance to earn a food treat. Horses are highly tuned in to seeking the next tasty morsel.

Teaching horses the click&treat dynamic is teaching them a novel way to forage. They quickly learn to relate a signal to a specific behavior which results in a food treat foraged. It is not so different from the foraging behaviors, other than grazing, that horses use in the wild:
- browsing on shrubs and trees
- stripping bark
- digging through snow
- when food is scarce, digging to expose edible roots
- hunting out late-melting snow in mountainous areas.

Clicker training is a 'pay as you go' process. Done correctly, it is highly motivating. If it is new to you, refer to Appendix 1 for information about how to effectively explore the possibilities of clicker training.

Some tasks of course, like haltering, saddling & harnessing, mounting & dismounting, worming, vet inspection, grooming and foot care, require the horse to stand still.

When we teach these standing still procedures, we begin with a release (click&treat) for relaxation during each tiny slice of the overall process. Gradually, as the horse can relax more, we do slightly more of the activity before each release (click&treat).

It's crucial to remember that standing still during an unusual situation is something a horse in the wild would never do.

Asking the horse to stand still while we do all sorts of things to him is a big ask. To teach a flight animal to stand still on request means we have to actively teach the horse to be inactive.

In other words, the horse learns to be 'actively inactive'. His instinct is to move if he feels uncomfortable. Careful training helps him gain the trust and confidence he needs to keep his feet still when we do things with him.

#20 HorseGym with Boots looks at this art of teaching 'active inactivity'.

Successive Approximations

In simple English, this means that we start with what the horse can offer already and gradually direct and reward each tiny change in the direction of the final behavior we want.

In other words, at the beginning of teaching something new, we release (click&treat) for the slightest approximation of what we want as our final result. Each improved approximation becomes one slice of the overall task.

When the horse feels ready, we encourage him to do a tiny bit more to gain the release (click&treat). This whole process of rewarding successive approximations is called 'shaping a behavior'.

A human example of shaping a behavior is teaching a child to write. We start with holding a pencil and using it to make random marks on paper. At some point the random marks become conscious curves and straight lines.

When the time is right, we introduce writing the letters of the alphabet. Eventually the child can group letters to make words. Words are then arranged into meaningful sentences. Some children go on to write coherent paragraphs, essays, stories or books.

If the child loses confidence with any of the slices of the process, an element of discomfort can creep in, along with typical avoidance behavior. Not enough practice then results in a poorly shaped skill.

Writing is an interesting human endeavor that starts at two years old and is still being shaped many years later at high school, university and beyond.

Another way to look at successive approximations is to think of a sculptor starting with a piece of stone. He works in careful stages until the shape in his mind is visible to the rest of us in the shape of the stone.

In the same way, we gradually tease a series of movements (or stillness) out of a horse to yield the task we want. This is a bit harder than shaping stone because horses have minds of their own.

An interesting study has appeared on www.appliedanimalbehaviour.com. It showed that horses can learn and use symbols to indicate their preferences.

Here is a brief description of the study. Using clicker training, 23 horses were taught the meanings of three visual posters. The poster graphics were:
- thick vertical black stripe on a white background for *cover off*
- thick horizontal black strip on a white background for *cover on*
- blank white sign for *no change*, which indicated that the horse either wanted to keep his cover on, or stay uncovered.

All the horses were used to wearing covers. They were stalled at night and turned out during the day. Their various owners decided when to put their covers on and when to take them off or leave them off.

The horses were taught one poster at a time. Once a horse was adept at targeting the *cover off* poster, he was given access to it with his cover on. When he targeted the poster, he earned his click&treat and his cover was immediately removed.

Then the horse was taught the *cover on* poster by earning a click&treat for targeting the poster, immediately followed by his cover being put on.

In the same way, the horse was taught to target the *no change* poster. If he had a cover on, nothing changed. If he was uncovered, he stayed that way.

There were many more intricate details that helped to keep the study as valid as possible. You can find them in the published paper noted in the reference section.

Evidently all 23 horses learned the tasks in 14 days with short training sessions almost every day.

On completion of training, horses overheated in their covers on a warm day clearly signaled they wanted their covers off.

Testing uncovered horses on cold, wet days when they showed signs of cold stress resulted in the horses clearly targeting that they wanted their covers on.

Horses tested in conditions where people assumed they were probably comfortable targeted the *no change* poster.

There were interesting peripheral observations, such as some of the horses becoming super keen to have their turn with the experimenters. No doubt they looked forward to the regular interaction and puzzle-solving involved to earn their carrot-strip treats.

Such eagerness to interact and learn new things is the most delightful outcome when we add clicker training to our horse activities.

General Key Points

1. The more quickly you take the pressure off (click&treat) when the horse complies, the faster the horse can learn to recognize just what it is you want.
2. Once the horse understands your intent, always start with the lightest signal possible, then add energy until you get a prompt response.
3. If you keep nagging with a light signal you will desensitize the horse and make him disregard the signal. Nagging is an easy habit to get into and hard to break.
4. For each horse, you have to experiment with the amount of energy (intensity) a signal needs to get the desired response. For sensitive, anxious horses, it might be very little. A bold, strong-minded horse might need stronger signal pressure at first while he works out what will result in the release (click&treat). <u>It is essential to stop or reduce the signal pressure as soon as the horse makes the choice that we want to reinforce</u>.
5. The energy you need to apply will also change with the situation and what you are asking the horse to do.

6. If you teach something with the free-shaping technique (see Chapter 4, *Clicker Training Logs* for the free-shaping of willing haltering), the horse learns without signal pressure to initiate an action. The horse does the action of his own free will. We mark the action with a click and reward it with a treat. Once the horse offers the behavior reliably, we can add a signal to it. The signal is usually determined by the nature of the task. For the haltering task, we start with the horse's natural curiosity about the hoop, and shape the haltering procedure from that.
7. Just when everything is feeling really good is the time to STOP. Avoid at all costs the urge to *do it again to see if we can*. Go do something relaxing instead.
8. One of the key skills of horsemanship is to read the horse accurately to be able to decide on the best signal to use at any one moment. It is part of the concept of 'feel'.

There is a section about developing 'feel in my book, *Conversations with Horses: An in-depth look at the Signals and Cues between Horses and their Handlers.*

When we watch a horse perform a complex task, it is not always easy to see the steps the handler took to reach the smooth end behavior. Even if we can find out how the horse was trained, that only tells us about what worked for that horse and that handler.

Here are some questions we'd have to ask ourselves.

- What did the horse know already before learning that task?
- How experienced is the handler?
- What method(s) of reinforcement does the handler use?
- How long have the horse and handler worked together?
- How long did it take them to reach this point?
- What were the tricky bits along the way?
- How often did the horse get confused?

- How often did the handler have to go back a few steps and work forward again?

Seeing a horse carrying out a task that grabs our fancy is the beginning of our own adventure. It gives us the inspiration to teach our horse something new. The starting point for any Plan and IEP will be unique to us.

Here is the definition of thin-slicing again.

Thin-slicing is a shorthand way of saying: split the overall task we want the horse to learn into its smallest teachable parts and teach each part in a way that makes it as easy as possible for the horse to understand.

Next, we'll look at how to write the *behavioral objectives* that will become the thin- slices of whatever task we have decided to teach.

ABCD: Writing Behavioral Objectives

A popular shorthand way to remember the features of good behavioral objectives is to learn the ABCD method outlined in the mind map, Figure 69.

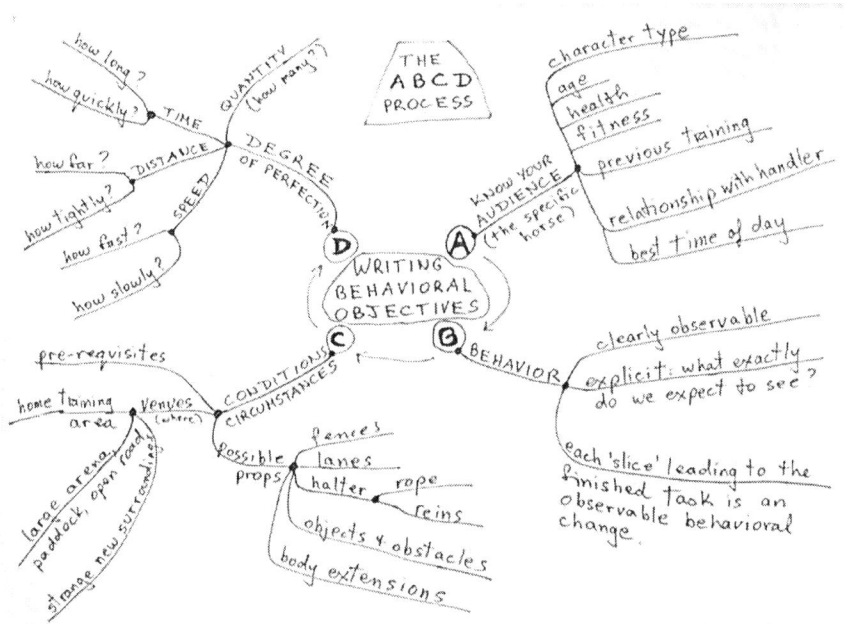

Figure 69: The ABCD Method of checking that we are writing good behavioral objectives.

I've drawn the mind map in Figure 69 with the horse in mind. It can apply equally if we are considering a handler. In the 'Behavior' branch, if we are considering ourselves, we can change '*what exactly do we expect to see?*' into '*what exactly will we do?* In other words, what will we actually do to communicate with the horse?

The **Audience** branch looks at the specifics of the horse we are planning for. It asks, "Who will be receiving this instruction?" The more detail we know about our **A**udience, the more refined our program can be. As mentioned earlier, as we teach our horse, we are also busy learning what works and what might benefit from adjustment.

If we are teaching many things to the same horse, our **A**udience will soon be well known. When we meet a new horse, we have to assess the various factors outlined in Figure 69. The more our IEP is tailored to the target **A**udience (specific horse), the more successful it will be.

The **Behavior** branch emphasizes that each objective we write clearly states an *observable* behavior. The more complex the overall task, the more slices it will have. Each slice is written as a behavioral objective.

Our job is to guide the horse from a vague approximation of the chosen task to its completion in a smooth and timely fashion. This is called shaping a behavior.

The **Conditions or Circumstances** branch makes sure that our program specifies where and when we expect the horse to be able to accomplish the task.

Conditions also include any props, obstacles, objects and body extensions we use to make it easier for the horse to understand what we want.

Usually, we gradually fade out the props and decrease the touch/gesture/rope/rein pressure as the horse gains a deeper understanding of what we are communicating.

Best training begins in an environment where the horse and handler are relaxed and distractions are manageable. If the horse can smoothly do the task in our usual training area, we've reached a certain level of competency.

If we want the horse to repeat the task,
- at a higher gait
- with more distractions
- in a new area
- with a different handler,

our program has to incorporate these changes in the conditions under which we want the horse to accomplish the task. I call this generalization.

Generalization enlarges the program to incorporate the behavioral objectives in other contexts. We want the horse to be able to do the task in different places and with different distractions. Depending on what we are teaching, the generalization may need a little bit more training time, or a great deal more training time.

If we have taught our horse to wear a saddle and be ridden in the comfortable atmosphere of our fenced arena at home, generalization to build confidence riding across irregular terrain and on public roads probably needs a new set of plans and IEPs.

Usually the handler also has to work on generalization. He or she may be able to communicate clearly with the horse in a quiet, private place. Doing the same in front of a group of people (especially naysayers) or in front of a camera may need thin-slicing and practice.

Degree of Perfection means that our behavioral objective has to include the measurable specifics of our expectation (e.g., how many, how long, how far, how fast).

Examples of *Quantity*:
1. Number of canter strides we would like after asking for a canter depart and before coming back to a trot.
2. If we are teaching our horse to count by pawing, how many pawing movements will earn a click&treat?
3. If we are doing suppling exercises over trotting poles, we may decide to ask for three repeats over four rails on a circle to the right.

Examples of *Time*:
1. A goal might be ten minutes of continuous working trot as part of a warm-up. We might start our program with three minutes and gradually work up to ten minutes.
2. If we want our horse to stay ground-tied, we start with half a second and work up to however long we'd like him to stay parked after we drop the lead rope. Chapter 8 develops a Training Plan for ground-tying.
3. If we want our horse to keep his nose placed on a target, we click&treat for one second, then two seconds, and so on until we reach the length of time we want.

Examples of *Distance*:
1. If we are teaching our horse to work in a circle around us, our first behavioral objective (slice) might be a quarter circle before we release (click&treat). As the horse gains confidence, we ask for a half circle, then

three-quarters of a circle, then a whole circle, then two circles, and so on.
2. If we are teaching backing with a hand signal, we may start with counting the number of steps back, then change to backing halfway across the arena, and so on.
3. If we are teaching the horse to move forward away from us to put his nose on a stationary target, or his feet on a mat, we will begin to send him from just a step or two away from the target, then gradually send him from further and further back.
4. If we are teaching our horse to travel confidently in a trailer, we may begin with driving across a paddock, graduate to going as far as the neighbor and back, then a short round-trip, a longer round-trip, and so on.
5. If we are teaching our horse to move through a narrow space, we start with the space relatively wide. The horse will tell us how wide it needs to be. As the horse gains confidence, we make the space narrower and narrower.

Examples of *Speed*:
1. If we are training a race horse, how fast he goes will determine his future.
2. If we do endurance riding, how fast we can go without over-stretching the horse's physical ability determines the winner.
3. If we are teaching our horse to spin, we start slowly and gradually ask for more speed.
4. In Horse Agility, obstacles are variously negotiated at walk, trot or canter.
5. In dressage, a pattern includes various gaits.
6. In a Western Equitation class, how slowly can our horse jog?
7. In show jumping, what is the speed of approach best suited to each obstacle?

From Task to Behavioral Objectives

Once we have clearly stated our task, we can begin the job of thin-slicing the overall task into its smallest teachable pieces.

When we are dealing with horse education, the only way to know whether we have achieved an objective is to take note of our own behavior and the behavior of the horse.

In other words, when we write our teaching program, we have to write each slice leading to the goal as a behavioural objective.

'Behavioral' means we have to use verbs (action words) that describe what we expect to see or feel as each slice leading to the goal is achieved.

We have to state the behaviors clearly and positively. In other words, we describe what we will be able to do. We don't describe what we don't want to happen.

This is really important, because we can't logically reinforce behaviors that we don't want. The objectives have to carefully state the behaviors we do want because they are the ones we will reinforce with release and reward.

Example of Slices Written as Behavioral Objectives

As an example, let's use one of the ways to teach a horse to step sideways. In the chart, the verbs (action words) for each behavior are underlined for each objective.

Figure 70: Sidestepping smoothly with a hand signal toward the ribs.

We'll write the task following the **ABCD** of writing good behavioral objectives.

- *Audience* = the horse
- *Behavior* = smoothly steps sideways, right or left
- *Conditions* = familiar learning environment; facing a fence that inhibits forward movement; in response to a gesture signal toward his girth area given with one hand (handler)
- *Degree of Perfection* = at least eight steps to right and left.

Task: In a familiar learning environment, while facing a fence that inhibits forward movement [**C**], the horse [**A**] sidesteps smoothly [**B**] for at least eight steps (to the right and the left) [**D**] when I give a gesture signal toward his girth area [**C**]. *#53 HorseGym with* Boots shows the teaching of this task.

The chart that follows has ten slices. For each slice, there is a description of what the handler's signals will look like, and what the horse's responses will look like. Because the task starts with the handler's action, the handler's action is written first on the chart.

The numbered statements describe the handler's behavior to give the signals. The next statement (H) is the horse's behavior that we want to reinforce with release (click&treat).

Thin-Slicing the Stepping Sideways Task

	Slices (Behavioral Objectives)	Tick
1	Breathes out & turns off body energy while facing the side of the horse in neutral.	
H	Stands quietly facing a fence.	
2	Breathes in & gestures toward or touches the horse's shoulder to ask the horse to yield his forequarters (F/Q); pauses to give horse time to move; click&treat for the yield.	
H	Yields the forequarters F/Q on request, given a gesture or touch signal toward the F/Q.	
3	Breathes in & gestures toward or touches the hindquarters (H/Q) to ask the horse to yield his H/Q; pauses to give horse time to move; click&treat for the yield.	
H	Yields the hindquarters H/Q on request, given a gesture or touch signal toward the H/Q.	
4	Breaths in & gestures or touches *alternate* between F/Q and H/Q to encourage the horse to move the front end and hind end rhythmically.	
H	Yields the F/Q and H/Q individually and rhythmically with alternating gesture or touch signals toward the horse's shoulder and hip.	
5	Breaths in & gestures or touches toward shoulder and hip *alternate more quickly* to ask for *continuous multiple sideways steps*.	
H	As H4, plus moves four sideways steps.	

6	As 5	
H	As H4, plus <u>moves</u> six sideways steps.	
7	As 5	
H	As H4, plus <u>moves</u> eight or more sideways steps.	
8	<u>Breaths in</u> & <u>gestures</u> or <u>touches</u> are *less pronounced*.	
H	<u>Moves</u> eight or more steps sideways when the gesture or touch signals aimed toward the shoulder and hip are less extreme.	
9	<u>Gestures</u>/<u>touches</u> at one spot at about the horse's girth line to ask for sideways steps (Figure 70).	
H	<u>Moves</u> eight or more steps sideways in response to one continuous-on signal at the girth area.	
10	<u>Signal</u> is clear on both the left and right sides of the horse.	
H	<u>Moves</u> eight or more steps equally well to the right and to the left.	

When we write a precise description for each *slice* of behavior that we want, our mind can more clearly see the following aspects of our training procedure. For example:
- what our signals (orientation, energy level, touch, gesture, voice) should be
- what precisely we want to see or feel the horse doing
- when we will remove our signal pressure (click&treat)
- where we need to slow down and spend more time.

Removing the signal pressure (click&treat) is the only way the horse can know when he is doing what we want. If we are clear and precise, two-way communication has opportunity to flourish.

The example above shows that we need to write behavioral objectives for both the horse and the handler.

Each slice of an over-all task has a handler component (how will I communicate what I want to the horse) and a horse component (what behavior will I reinforce?).

Two-way Communication

When we ask the horse to do something, we are speaking. When the horse responds with the movement (or stillness) that we requested, he is speaking. We say, "Please do this." He says, "Okay, I know how to do that."

If we are teaching something new, we say, "Please try this and I'll click&treat (or release the signal pressure) when you make a good effort."

If we are together at liberty, and the horse decides to leave us, he is saying, "I'd rather do something else." If we are listening, we'll say, "Okay, I'll do something else as well," and move away in the opposite direction to the horse. Communication to disagree is just as valid as communication to agree.

The horse can speak first and we can listen. When Boots decides to leave the liberty game we are playing, I move away and busy myself moving an obstacle or walking around enjoying the view. Usually Boots soon moseys over to join me again and we continue with whatever we were doing or play with something new.

Out walking with halter and lead, Boots often stops beside one of her favorite grassy areas to remind me that she'd like a nibble. I listen and often we pause for a bit of grazing.

Eventually I ask her to walk on and she complies. Sometimes I hear what she is asking, but decide not to stop.

When two beings are together, one usually suggests what they will do next. With our horses, we usually decide, but as we learn to listen to our horses more carefully, there are times when we can and should let them make a decision.

Chapters 7 and 8 look at two more examples of Training Plan and Individual Education Program creation. The examples we'll use are teaching the weave pattern and ground-tying.

Boots is ground-tied as I set up the camera to film weaving a circle of cones.

Chapter 7
Writing Training Plans and IEPs
The difference between Training Plans and IEPs

The Training Plan defines the overall task as a clear behavior or series of behaviors that we would like our horse to achieve. We develop the plan by breaking the whole task into its smallest teachable pieces. This is the process of 'thin-slicing'.

We then create an Individual Education Program (IEP) by taking the thin-sliced Training Plan and incorporating the following:
- specific horse's character type
- handler's experience & personality
- venues available
- objects and obstacles available
- time available
- simulations appropriate
- reinforcement techniques.

An Individual Education Program (IEP) is designed to suit a specific horse and handler combination, as well as the time and the specific training facilities available.

We might be writing an IEP for ourselves and our own horse. If we are mentoring other people, we may write a Training Plan and possible IEP for another handler and horse combination, until they are experienced enough to write their own.

There are a variety of approaches to writing plans, but they all share similarities.

How Horses do Thin-Slicing

Since we are training horses, it makes sense to look first at how horses create Training Plans for themselves.

Often people see something they would like their horse to do and try to directly re-create what they saw. Horses are more circumspect.

If we set up a spooky object in the horse's home area while they are not there, we can observe their reactions when they return and first see the spooky thing.

Their bodies instantly switch into high alert. If the item is spooky enough, they move away from it until they feel safe enough to turn, face it, and reconsider.

If the spooky object does not give chase, the bolder horses approach a little way, then retreat again. Gradually each approach gets closer to the spooky object and each retreat is shorter.

If nothing happens to spook the horses further, the boldest horse eventually puts his whiskers on the spooky object or he may check it out by pawing.

If we watch closely, we can see the moment a horse makes the decision that he can relax with a new object. His body relaxes, his head comes down, he may lick and chew, and he returns to grazing, resting, or his social engagements.

Other horses in the group do a similar exploration or they accept the decision of the bolder horse and relax when he or she relaxes.

So we can see that horses naturally thin-slice the task of confidence-building about anything unusual in their environment. Here is a summary.
1. Retreat to a distance which allows them to feel safe enough to stop, turn and reconsider.
2. Advance to the edge of their comfort zone and observe the spooky object.
3. If nothing happens to reignite their flight response, their comfort zone expands and they advance a bit more.
4. Repeat slice 3 until they are comfortable enough to put their nose or foot on the object to check it out.
5. Make a decision. The horses will decide that there is danger and move away or they may decide that there is no danger and accept the presence of the unusual new item.

6. Carry on with everyday life: grazing, browsing, social interactions and resting.

If we model our Training Plans and Individual Education Programs (IEPs) on horses' natural approach to new learning, we start with a big advantage.

The key is to begin from a place of safety and confidence, and work toward a goal in slices small enough to maintain safety and confidence.

Thin-Slicing Revisited

The first step of thin-slicing is a brainstorm to dissect the overall task into its smallest teachable parts. Some people call this 'task analysis'. Then we organize these components or slices into an order that makes sense to us and will hopefully make sense to the horse.

Each slice is a clear description of an observable behavior that we can see (or feel) when the horse achieves it.

We also describe the behaviors we will use to clearly signal our intent to the horse. Each slice has a horse dimension and a handler dimension.

The 'Progress Log for Teaching/Learning Willing Haltering' in the Chapter 4 section about *Clicker Training Logs'* is an example of thin slices written for both the horse and the handler. Because the horse initiates the behavior, the horse's behavior is written first in the chart.

On the chart, *Thin-Slicing the Stepping Sideways Task* in Chapter 6, the handler's behavioral objective is written first because the handler initiates this task.

Once you thin-slice the task, you'll have an idea about where your release/click points will *probably* be for each slice. These may change once you actually begin with the horse.

Feedback from the horse and your own reactions will always affect what you do next.

The main idea is to keep the horse being successful, i.e., earning frequent release (click&treat) as much as possible. If an attempt gets fluffed up (by you or the horse), pause, relax and reset the slice you are working on. Alternatively, you may decide that the best way forward is to back up in the program to an earlier slice.

As long as the horse is willing to try again, nothing is lost. If we get frustrated the horse feels it in a nanosecond and will become anxious.

A good way to avoid that feeling of frustration is to pretend it went well, smile and breathe out. With practice, it becomes easier to relax and calmly reset the task.

Working with thin-slicing means carefully checking (and rechecking) that the horse is comfortable and confident with each tiny slice of the process before moving on.

It pays to remember that the *process* of teaching does not look like the finished product.

One horse may learn something in five minutes the first time we teach it. Another horse may take days, weeks or months to reach the same level of confidence and physical expertise.

We have to balance the need to build confidence around each slice, with the need to move on when we should, so the horse doesn't get bored. It's never easy to walk the fine line between moving too fast and going too slowly.

Pacing our training for good results gets easier with:
- experience
- understanding a particular horse's character type
- reading the horse carefully
- becoming more aware of our own body language
- becoming more aware of our emotional state
- getting adept at resetting tasks.

When we use the thin-slicing technique, we may find that one horse easily moves through the basic slices very quickly and we are soon working on more challenging parts of the task.

Every time we start a new task, it's important to not presume we know what the horse already understands. He may know more than we think, or he may know less.

Instead, we quietly work through all the slices in our plan, starting with the easiest, most basic requests. When we reach the edge of the horse's comfort zone (or ours), we slow down.

Each horse will have different comfort zone edges, as will each handler. The same horse (and handler) will have different comfort zones for different tasks and in different environments.

The next horse we present with the same task may be missing an understanding of the most basic prerequisites necessary, so we expand our IEP to cover them as well.

Since each horse/human partnership is unique, there are no recipes or 'one size fits all' patterns.

Whatever the horse is doing when he feels the release and/or hears the click (followed by a treat) is what he will note as the correct thing to do in that situation. If our timing is inconsistent, we are making things harder than they need to be, both for ourselves and for the horse.

Timing can be improved with focus and physical practice. Once we can recognize the moments when our timing is off, we can apologize to the horse and strive to do better next time.

It is fun to practice timing when we watch TV. For a few minutes of viewing, choose something specific to click with a clicker. Or squeeze a soft ball or tap a pencil every time an actor smiles, a car comes on screen or the ball reaches the rim of the basket during a basketball game.

If that annoys the person watching with you, get them to do it too! We can improve our powers of observation as well as our hand-eye coordination many-fold with short, regular bursts of timing training.

Writing a Training Plan

1. Deciding on the Training Topic

First, we have to decide on a behavior set that we would like to work with. Your topic decisions will obviously be influenced by what you want to do, for example:

- improve every-day handling skills (loose-rope leading, politeness around food, foot care, moving safely through gates, getting used to leaving home, trailer loading and traveling, vet care)
- keep the horse moving regularly (walking out or riding)
- enjoyment via simple hacking out or trail riding
- have fun with tricks (bowing, smiling, counting, retrieving, leg lifts)
- play with gymnastic exercises for overall fitness (trotting poles, hills, weaving)
- teach a skill set needed for a competitive discipline (show-jumping, dressage, equitation, reining, polo, gymkhanas, driving, showing 'in hand')
- teach specific requirements for a competition (trail obstacles, Horse Agility)
- develop the confidence a horse needs to work with disadvantaged or novice people.

2. Scoping the Topic

For my example topic, I've chosen teaching the horse to weave a series of objects. It's a useful gymnastic exercise that's not too easy or too hard.

The basic weaving task can be generalized in several ways. Weaving comes in two groundwork formats. One has the handler weaving with the horse and the other has the horse weaving while the handler does not.

The weave is also useful for riding. It's a suppling exercise for the horse and works nicely as a body language exercise for the handler.

'Scoping the topic' means getting your head around all the things that the topic might include. It also helps you to think about the prerequisites that the tasks require.

Once you've scoped the topic you may find that you have to backtrack and begin with a Training Plan and IEP for a skill that your horse doesn't have yet, but which is needed as a foundation for the task you have in mind.

A handy way to do this is with a mind map as in Figure 71. A mind map is one way to get all your ideas onto a piece of paper as quickly as possible. As you reflect on the subject matter and rewrite the mind map, new connections between topics often become apparent.

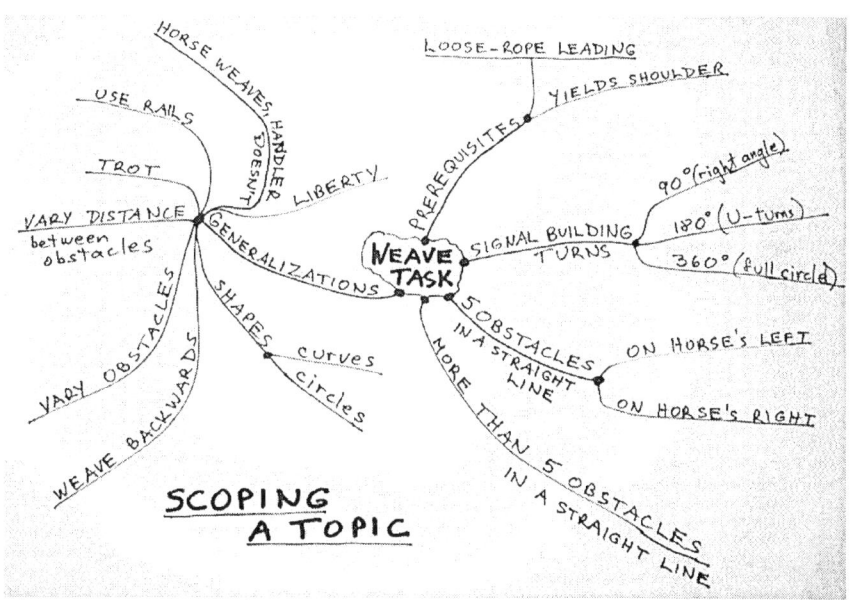

Figure 71: A 'scoping' mind map links general ideas that relate to the task we've decided to work with. This is my third version. Coming back to it over several days gives the brain time to mull things over and make new connections.

The mind map in Figure 71 includes prerequisites and generalizations. It outlines basic skills we can use to build up the horse's suppleness and his understanding of our body language.

It reminds us that we have to develop clear body language signals that indicate when we want the horse to 'draw' toward us and when we want him to yield his shoulder away from us.

Once you are happy with your scoping mind map, it's time to decide on and write down the overall task you want to begin with. The overall task is usually made up of a series of individual behaviors chained together.

3. Thin-Slicing the Overall Task into Behavioral Objectives

In Chapter 6 we looked at details about the **ABCD** method of writing *behavioral objectives* (see Figure 69). Once you have a clear idea about the nature of your **A**udience (your horse) you can follow the rest of the **ABCD** technique in order to quickly work out whether you have clearly defined:

- the exact **B**ehavior you want
- the **C**onditions under which you will ask for the behavior
- the **D**egree of Proficiency or Perfection that you want.

The **A**udience for your teaching is your horse with all his quirks. If we are helping someone else with a horse, they and their horse are our **A**udience.

If things are not going to plan, usually we have to look to ourselves and change what we are doing. When we hit the right notes, the horse magically gets better at what we are asking him to do.

For some things, the **D**egree of Proficiency or Perfection is fairly flexible. If you are leading your horse in a casual way, it might not matter if his nose is beside you, slightly in front or slightly behind, as long as there is slack in the lead rope and he is walking with you willingly.

For other things, the **D**egree of Proficiency or Perfection is important for safety or general care. When you show up with a bucket of feed, you always want the horse to wait until he is released to the food rather than have him pushing into you as soon as he sees the bucket.

When you ask the horse to pick up a foot for cleaning or trimming, you expect it to happen every time unless the horse is injured or you forgot to make sure he is standing squarely.

4. The Basic Weave Task Defined

Here is my wording for the basic weaving task. Stating the task like this sets the framework within which the training will be carried out.

Defined Task: In our usual training environment, the horse and I, moving together shoulder-to-shoulder, cleanly weave five objects set in a straight line. We can do it with me walking on either side of the horse.

Note that I've paid attention to the **ABCD** for writing good behavioral objectives.

Audience = my horse

Behavior = weave objects moving together

Conditions = usual training environment, objects in a straight line, shoulder-to-shoulder leading position

Degree of proficiency = 5 objects, cleanly, leading on either side of the horse

Figure 72: Weaving obstacles in a row.

At this point, I find that a mind map showing further detail about the defined task is useful. *Breaking the task down further is the process of thin-slicing.* Ideally, each branch of the mind map ends in slices thin enough to describe individual observable behaviors.

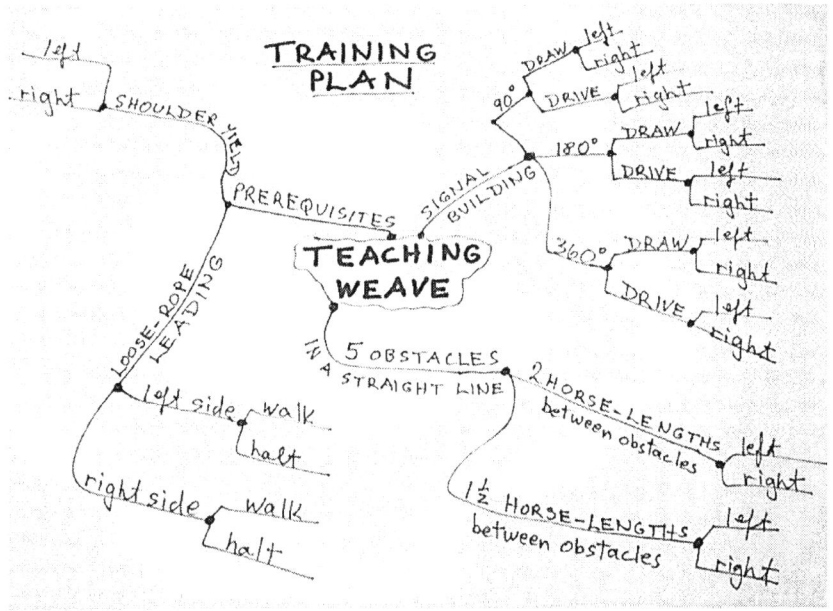

Figure 73: This mind map of the basic weave task expands each branch outward until the smallest branches are a discrete 'slice' that can be stated as a behavioral objective. In other words, each branch-end is an observable behavior which we can look for and reinforce.

'Draw' is when the horse is turning toward the handler and 'drive' is when the horse is turning away from the handler. 'Left' and 'right' indicate which side of the horse the handler is walking on.

#67-71 HorseGym with Boots (inclusive) show the slices in action. Viewing the clips makes it easier to get a mental picture of the overall process.

We can use a chart to outline the slices of the task. The chart that follows sets out a series of possible slices (*behavioral objectives*) that can be used to teach the weave task. Some helpful illustrations follow the chart.

Reminders and hints for the handler are incorporated within the chart. The numbered items are the slices - what we want to see the horse doing.

Slices of the Weave Task Written as Behavioral Objectives

Slices (behavioral objectives)	Achieved
1. Horse walks at least 20 meters shoulder-to-shoulder with the handler; relaxed; draped lead; with handler on the horse's *left side*.	
2. As 1 but handler is on the horse's right side.	
➢ Teach on both sides: most horses (and people) find these exercises harder on one side. The handler will find it harder to activate smooth signals on one side of his or her body. The horse will find it harder to flex horizontally in one direction. This is due to our natural asymmetry and is totally normal. If we work a little bit more often on the harder side, the differences will gradually become less noticeable.	
➢ Handler Signals: 'Draw': Hips & shoulder (body axis) turned slightly away from the horse and head leaned away. Start large & obvious; tone down as horse becomes savvy. ➢ Touch signal behind if the horse lags. Because the horse has further to go than the handler, be careful to take small steps <u>but keep your energy up</u> so he doesn't 'stall out'. See Figure 74.	
➢ Handler Signals: 'Drive': Hips & shoulder (body axis) turned slightly toward the horse and head leaned toward the horse. Maybe add a hand or body extension gesture toward the head when the horse is first learning. Start large & obvious; tone down as horse becomes savvy. See Figure 75. ➢ Some horse character types are reluctant to yield their front end, so if this is sticky with your horse, devise a Plan and IEP to address it separately. ➢ My *Thin Slicing Examples* playlist has a clip called <u>Shoulder Yield into a Turn on the Haunches</u> which may be helpful.	

➢ Timing your steps to the horse's movement is important. If you go too fast, you'll get ahead of him and stall him out. He'll probably dodge behind you. If you go too slowly, he will get too far ahead and may squeeze away in front of you. So for teaching, adjust your speed to the horse's natural gait.	
3. Horse cleanly steps 90-degrees (right angle turn) around an obstacle; *handler is between the horse and the obstacle*, 'drawing' the horse around; handler on *left side of horse*.	
4. As 3 but the handler is on the horse's right side.	
5. Horse fluidly moves his shoulder 90-degrees around an obstacle; when the *horse is between the obstacle and the handler*, so the handler is 'driving' the horse around; handler on *left side of horse*.	
6. As 5 but the handler is on the horse's right side.	
7. Horse stays shoulder-to-shoulder with the handler as the handler 'draws' him into a 180-degree U-turn around an obstacle; the *handler is between the obstacle and the horse*; handler on *left side of horse*.	
8. As 7 but the handler is on the horse's right side.	
9. Horse stays shoulder-to-shoulder with the handler as the handler 'drives' him into a 180-degree U-turn around an obstacle; the *horse is between the obstacle and the handler*; handler on *left side of horse*.	
10. As 9 but the handler is on the horse's right side.	
11. Horse stays shoulder-to-shoulder with the handler as the handler 'draws' him into a 360-	

degree (full turn) around an obstacle; the *handler is between the obstacle and the horse*; handler on *left side of horse.*

12. As 11 but the handler is on the horse's right side.

13. Horse stays shoulder-to-shoulder with the handler as the handler 'drives' him into a 360-degree (full turn) around an obstacle; the *horse is between the obstacle and the handler*; handler on *left side of horse.*

14. As 13 but the handler is on the horse's right side.

15. Horse stays shoulder-to-shoulder with the handler as the handler 'draws' and 'drives' him in a figure eight pattern around two obstacles; for one obstacle, the handler will be between the obstacle and the horse (draw). For the other obstacle, the horse will be between the obstacle and the handler (drive); handler on *left side of horse.* See Figures 78 and 79.

16. As 15 but the handler is on the horse's right side.

- ➤ MAJOR MILESTONE: Once the horse is tuned in to your signals for the 90, 180 and 360-degree turns, he will usually find it easy to understand your body orientation signals in order to weave a series of obstacles in a straight line.
- ➤ You have also taken him through a flexion program that has strengthened his muscles and joints.
- ➤ Gradually reduce the intensity of your signals to see how small you can get them.
- ➤ Destinations: if your horse is savvy about nose or foot targets, having one at either end of your weave will give him extra motivation to do the weave because he already knows where his next release (click&treat) spot is.

17. Horse stays shoulder-to-shoulder with the handler as the handler moves with the horse to alternately draw and drive around a series of five objects set out in a row; two horse-lengths between the objects; handler on *left side of horse*. See Figures 76 and 77.

18. As 17 but the handler is on the horse's right side.

19. As 17 but decrease the distance between objects to one-and-a-half horse-lengths; handler on *left side of horse*.

20. As 19 but the handler is on the horse's right side.

> **Generalizations**: in this case the generalizations might not need a whole Plan and IEP of their own. As usual, teach everything on both sides of the horse.

1. Repeat 17 at trot.

2. Weave a larger number of obstacles in a straight line. See Figure 80.

3. Set the obstacles in a curve.

4. Set the obstacles in a circle; large circle at first, then reduce the size.

5. Use different obstacles: tubs, buckets, barrels upright, barrels on their sides, large cones, small cones, bottles of water, tread in posts, tires, stones, rags, hunks of firewood, cardboard boxes. If out and about, you might be able to use trees, shrubs, bollards, cars, willing people, nicely spaced weeds or cow poos.

6. Set up a weave on a slope; up and down or along the slope.

7. Put rails between the obstacles so the horse is developing hock flexion as well as horizontal flexion.

8. Vary the spaces between the obstacles.	
9. Have some space with rails and some without.	
10. Build a circle of rails laying on the ground, leaving gaps between the ends of the rails. Weave the gaps or weave crossing the center of each rail.	
11. Using a circle of markers, send the horse to weave them, moving your feet as little as possible; ultimately stand still in the center.	
12. Teach weaving backwards. Your position will probably be in front of the horse, facing him. Teach three signals: backwards straight, hind end to left and hind end to right. Use large obstacles like barrels or tall cones or big cardboard boxes that the horse can see easily.	
13. Play with all of it at liberty.	
14. Starting slowly, have only the horse weave the obstacles while the handler walks alongside.	
15. As 14 at trot.	

Weave Illustrations

It's much easier to visualize the parts of a task if we see photos and video clips, so I've included pictures to illustrate some of the slices.

Figure 74: The 'Draw': I'm between the horse and the barrel. To 'draw' Boots around the barrel, I take short, active steps. She has to move further than I do, so I keep my body energy high to help her keep up her rhythm as she moves around the barrel.

My body language signal for the 'draw' in Figure 74 consists of turning my outside shoulder and hip slightly away from the horse and tilting my head to the outside. I also use the voice signal, "Around" to let her know we are going to turn around the barrel.

The pictures show us using a barrel. It makes more sense to the horse to go around something large. To keep up enthusiasm for the task, I release the horse to a target mat for a click&treat. At first, we go to the mat after every turn, then after a few turns. Eventually I phase out the mat in favour of a 'triple treat' for a good sustained effort.

A triple treat is a small break in the concentration of learning a task. I ask Boots to target my outstretched fist three times in a row, with a click&treat after each one. *#16 HorseGym with Boots* illustrates the 'triple treat'.

You can use a single object like a barrel to do:

- the 90-degree (right-angle) turns
- the 180-degree U-turns
- the 360-degree full turns around the object.

#67 HorseGym with Boots shows us using a square of ground rails for the 90-degree turns. I like to teach each concept using as many different objects or obstacles as possible.

We can make the 'draw' and 'drive' sessions more interesting by setting out a circuit of objects and varying the type of turn we do at each one. Using circuits is a way to generalize the concept in the horse's mind.

Figure 75: The 'Drive': The horse is between me and the barrel, which means I'm asking her to move her shoulder away from me as we move around the barrel. My body language signal is to turn my outside shoulder a little bit toward her. If the horse does not understand the shoulder-yield exercise, we need to teach it separately as a prerequisite. My body language is exaggerated in the photo so it is easier to see my body language signals.

Whenever you begin a new task, you are experimenting to find the signals that arise naturally out of the task and make sense to you and the horse. Sometimes it takes a while to get them consistent and smooth.

Once you've decided on your signals, frequent consistent practice in small bursts puts them into your muscle memory and the horse's deep memory. Once the horse is clear about your 'draw' and 'drive' signals for these large turns, weaving is usually a straightforward exercise.

Figure 76: The 'draw' as we weave through a set of five obstacles set in a straight line. My shoulder, hip and head are turned away from the horse. As soon as we pass the cone, we move into our 'drive' signal to make it around the next cone. Figures 76 and 77 show how much bend a horse has to engage when the cones are about one-and-a-half horse-lengths apart.

Figure 77: The 'drive' as we navigate a straight row of five obstacles. My outside shoulder is turned toward the horse and my head is tilted toward her. The 'head tilt' will eventually be the key signal. I'm giving a gesture signal with my outside hand to encourage her front end to bend away from me.

When we can smoothly weave five or six obstacles in a straight line, we can begin to generalize the task.

Figure 78: Practicing 'Draw' and 'Drive' by walking a figure eight between two objects. If I'm on the horse's right side, as above, we 'draw' around the object on the left side of the picture and 'drive' around the object on the right side of the picture, as shown in Figure 79.

Figure 79: 'Driving' around the second obstacle for our figure eight pattern. It's good to do a little bit of this exercise often. This is a gymnastic exercise to help the horse keep supple, but we don't want to make him sore.

In the foreground of Figure 79 you can see the mat where we go for relaxation (click&treat) after a good effort. When I first introduce this exercise, I put the mat in the center between the two obstacles to provide a high rate of reinforcement, i.e. after each turn.

Figure 80: Generalizing to different objects and to more of them in a line.

Writing Individual Education Programs (IEPs)

Before we look at the things to consider as we write an IEP, let's have a look at the advantages of starting with such a detailed written program. Once it is in writing, it's easy to tweak and adjust the program according to the feedback we gain during our sessions with the horse.

What an IEP does for the Horse

1. It takes his character type into consideration.
2. It takes into consideration his previous training and background experiences as much as it is possible to know them.
3. It presents information and expectations in slices small enough to enable him to understand what we want.
4. It tries hard to allow him to be continually successful.
5. It ensures that he learns each slice of a task thoroughly before moving on. The timeline is based on the horse's progress, not a date on a calendar or our expectations from experiences with other horses.
6. It incorporates objects and obstacles that make it easier for him to carry out the desired behavior.
7. It constructs a complex task by gradually chaining together the individual parts of the task.
8. If confidence fails, a written program makes it easy to go back and find a slice where we can re-establish confidence.
9. It maintains the horse's willingness to try new things.
10. It maintains the horse's willingness to improve things he knows.
11. It encourages the horse to look forward to training sessions.
12. It stops the horse from having to cope with the handler's fumbling with new skills if the handler has a clear idea of what she or he is doing, and has practiced mechanical skills away from the horse.

What an IEP does for the Handler
1. It highlights the skills the handler needs in order to communicate clearly with the horse to achieve a particular goal.
2. It suggests simulations the handler can use to gain or improve the mechanics of the handling skills needed for the task.
3. It includes a reasonable time frame.
4. It includes the venues available.
5. It includes consideration of the horse's character type, age, health, previous training and previous experiences.
6. It outlines the objects and obstacles that can be used to make it easier for the horse to carry out the desired behaviors while in the learning stage.
7. It lays out a possible order of thin-slices that lead to the final complex behavior.
8. It causes the hander to think carefully about the signals and body orientations that may work best to communicate intent.
9. It makes it easier to back up in the program if the horse shows anxiety or lack of confidence with a particular slice of the work.
10. It maintains motivation because we always start with what we *can do* and move forward in tiny slices from there.
11. It includes the four main stages of learning (see Appendix 2 for details). These are:
    - acquisition
    - fluidity
    - generalization
    - maintenance.
12. It makes it easy to know where we are in our program.
13. It allows us to look back at how we began and trace our path to the present point in the training.

14. It gives us a written record that we can adapt for different horses.

The basis of each Individual Education Program (IEP) is a thin-sliced Training Plan. The IEP can only be written by the handler of the horse. It expands the Training Plan by considering the unique situation of a specific horse and handler.

What makes sense to any particular horse will depend on his:

- innate character type
- genetic predispositions
- age
- health
- fitness
- previous life experiences that built up his confidence
- previous life experiences that drained his confidence
- what the horse knows already in relation to the task; he might know a lot or very little indeed.

What makes sense to the horse will also depend on how we present each new slice of the task. The handler's personality and teaching approach is hugely significant. The horse is obviously also influenced by the following factors.

1. The horse immediately picks up the handler's emotional state. Horses are probably comfortable with emotional neutrality but seem to thrive with cheerfulness.
2. If the handler has good control of his or her energy levels, energy level becomes a meaningful signal and the horse can learn to match his energy to that of the handler.
3. If the handler is able to temporarily set aside life's tensions and engage with mindfulness in the horse's more timeless approach to life, dwelling in the moment rather than the past or the future, it's possible for the horse to relax in the handler's company.

4. If the handler can 'pretend' it went well, remove pressure, smile, count to ten and reset an exercise when it goes awry, the horse is not made to feel wrong. The horse will usually willingly try again. The 'pretending' might seem bizarre at first, but it allows us to smile and it strongly counterbalances our natural tendency to get frustrated. It is a learned response we can build into our training technique.

The short section below called Patience Technique is borrowed from my book, *Walking with Horses: The Eight Leading Positions*.

Patience Technique

It's helpful to teach ourselves a patience technique. This can be a struggle at first. It may require quite a mental shift in how we perceive our horse and what we are asking him to do.

Patience techniques can include some or all of the responses listed below. As soon as we feel the first hint of frustration, we can do things like:
- consciously breathing out
- turning our energy off; maybe turn away from the horse
- rolling our shoulders to relax them
- taking up a neutral body stance that will become our default position whenever we feel frustration starting up or need to give the horse time to return to relaxation
- remembering that we have taken the horse out of his normal herd life and expect him to put up with things a horse living naturally would never come across
- smiling as we realize we've just done the right thing by defusing our tension or frustration rather than letting it influence our actions
- counting numbers until the frustration fades away
- decide to quietly finish the session.

First, we become mindful that we can lower our frustration rate by doing things like these. Eventually we may remember to apply them more and more while we are out with the horse.

Hints for Writing Your IEPs

An Individual Education Program is always a *work in progress* and usually we go back and tweak it many times. Sometimes we throw the whole thing out and start again.

Each time you work with your horse, you get additional feedback from the horse and from your own reactions and responses.

When we want to teach something new, the first step is to experiment, in a low-key way, to see what the horse can offer already in relation to the new goal we have in mind.

The experimentation gives us an idea about where our Individual Education Program (IEP) needs to start. We want to base new tasks on foundation training that the horse is already confident with. If the foundation is missing or shaky, we know where we have to start.

Our first job will be to write and execute IEPs to ensure that the horse has a solid foundation of basic skills. Then we can set new challenges to keep alive his curiosity and interest.

Before you begin to write your IEP, you will have:

- decided on the task you want to work on
- thin-sliced the task into your own Training Plan or found an existing Training Plan that you can adapt
- checked in with your horse about the task, i.e. what does he know already and what is missing
- decided on an appropriate starting point for your horse.

Once you've found a starting point, you can begin to write your IEP. You can change the thin-slicing of the Training Plan any time to make it a better fit for your horse and your training style.

Consider how often you can train. If your horse lives at your place and you can pop out three times a day for a mini-session, things can progress rapidly. If your horse is boarded and you see him daily, things can also progress rapidly.

If you can only visit your horse once a week, things may go a bit more slowly. In other words, you need to add a time and opportunity strand into your IEP.

What works for one horse may not work for another, so each horse needs his own IEP. If you work with many horses teaching the same skills, you will develop the facility to devise IEPs in your head almost immediately.

It's easy to have too few slices in an IEP but we can never have too many.

The more easily the horse can move from tiny slice to tiny slice, the easier it is for him to be continually successful and wanting to do more. Success builds on success.

My Balloon Popping IEP took a lot of revision before I had Boots confidently popping balloons with her foot. My friend's horse, Smoky, loved the exercise from the beginning and would hunt for balloons to pop. Each horse is unique.

A clip called *Smoky Bursts Balloons* in my *Single Obstacle Challenges* playlist shows how keenly Smoky enjoyed the game.

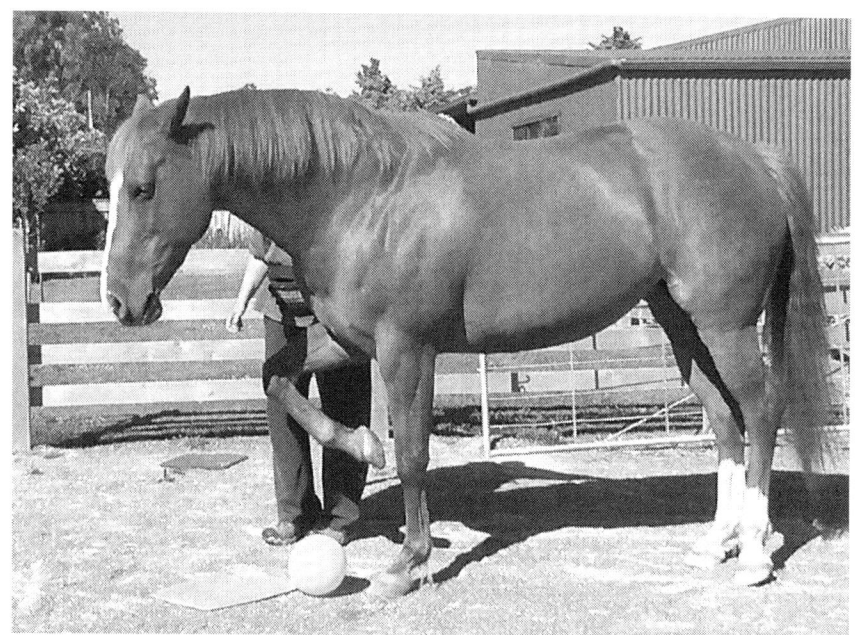

Figure 81: Popping balloons: Boots and I went through quite a few versions of our IEP before we got to the stage of easily popping balloons for fun. Keeping the balloon in one place so she could target it accurately was a major logistical challenge. Taping the balloon to a board makes it easier.

In this chapter, I've presented a Training Plan for teaching a horse to weave obstacles. That's as far as I can go.

Writing an Individual Education Program for yourself and a specific horse is the next step and only you can take that step. You may decide to follow my Training Plan or maybe you already teach the weave successfully using a different approach.

Once you've written your first Training Plan and IEP, it gets easier each time you do another one. While you are thinking about how to approach a task, draw up a mind map. Revise and add to the mind map over several days. A bad idea that you experimented with and rejected is just as valuable as a good idea that works well.

Chapter 8 looks at a second example of how to develop a task. We'll look at teaching our horse to ground-tie.

Chapter 8

A Training Plan for Ground-Tying

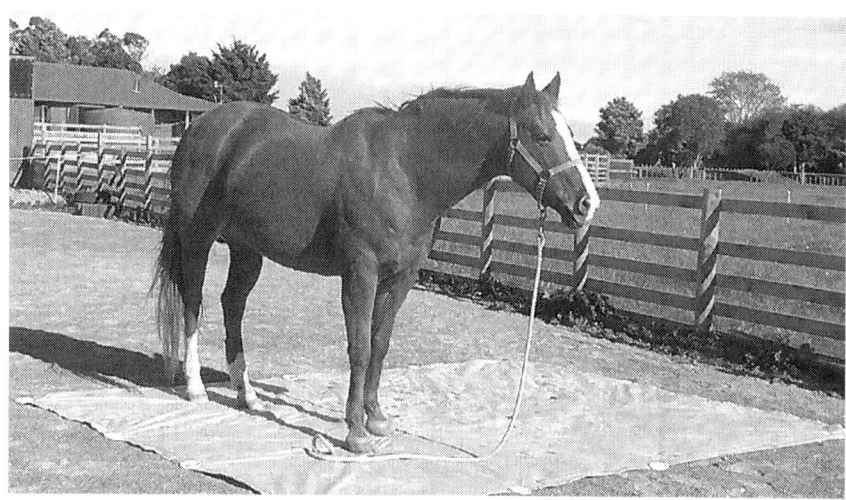

Figure 82: Ground-tying is a skill that is useful in many situations.

I've chosen ground-tying as the context for our second example because it is a specific skill useful for any horse. The prerequisite skills include:
- confidently wearing a halter (see Chapter 4, *Clicker Training Logs*, Example One: Willing Haltering)
- able to stand still in relaxed mode while things are happening around him
- stopping willingly at a preset mat destination
- smooth walk on and halt transitions staying beside the handler
- nice back up with the handler beside the horse or facing the front of the horse
- willing response to a voice "Whoa" signal
- rope relaxation and rope calmness in various situations (see Prerequisite E).

Having a horse stop and wait when a lead rope is dropped onto the ground is useful for management around home as well as out on the trail. It pops up occasionally as a challenge in Horse Agility competitions.

Safety:

My preference is to use a wide webbing or leather halter. If the horse moves, steps on his rope and reacts by jerking his head up, there is less chance of spinal trauma. To my mind, rope halters are not for tying up or ground-tying.

I also suggest using a soft, thick rope not longer than 12 feet. If the horse does move, it's better if there isn't a long, thin rope chasing him.

We have to make sure that the horse is totally relaxed with ropes dragging all around his body and legs. He has to be cool with ropes moving in front of him, behind him and dragging alongside while attached to his halter. Rope Relaxation is covered in detail as 'Prerequisite D' coming up in this chapter.

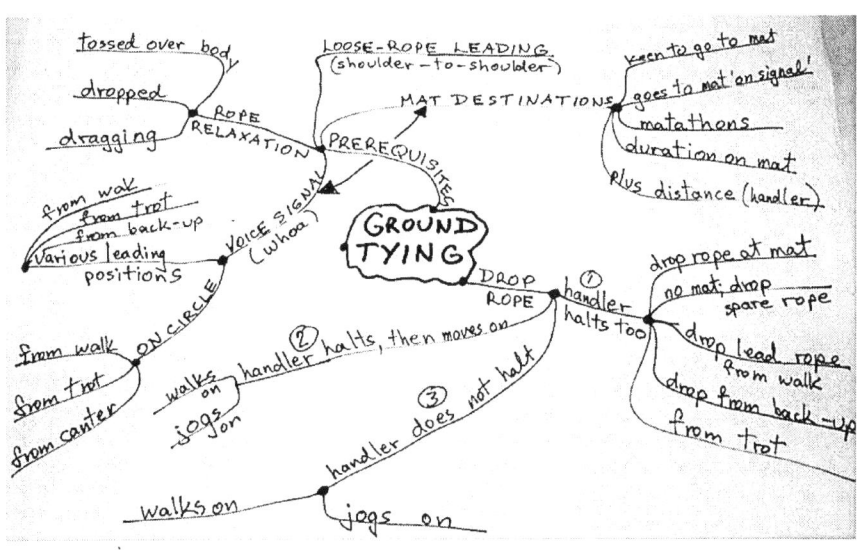

Figure 83: Mind map for the Ground-tying topic.

The term 'matathons' refers to setting out a number of mats and asking the horse to do something different at each one. *#11 HorseGym with Boots* illustrates a matathon.

The Prerequisites

A. Standing Still – Teaching Parking

First, let's look at the importance of standing still, since ground-tying is a standing- still task.

Horses don't stand still unless they are resting or scanning the environment to see if all remains safe in their surroundings. So, when we want to ask a horse working with us to stand still, it is a behavior that we have to carefully teach.

Nature doesn't supply piles of hay, so grazing or browsing keeps horses moving along one step at a time, or walking to seek more food.

Horses evolved on sparse steppe or prairie grasslands. Nowadays many feral horses survive in marginal desert or mountainous regions. Finding enough calories to stay alive is a constant challenge, especially during winter snows and summer droughts.

Equally important, summer grazing has to be carried out within reach of water or late-melting snowbanks in mountainous country. So, horses in the wild are forced to move a great deal every day.

Which brings us back to our point. It's a major learning task for a horse to stand quietly when we ask him to:
- be tied up
- travel in a vehicle
- stand on a mat
- stand beside a nose target
- be ground-tied.

We are teaching a complex, unnatural behavior, so it helps to take the time it needs to teach standing still carefully and thoroughly. I like to call it parking. *#20 HorseGym with Boots* is on the topic of parking.

There are all sorts of reasons we want our horse to stay parked, meaning that he stands still confidently, without needing to be tied up. Relaxed parking is useful for:
- grooming
- foot care
- massage
- vet procedures
- dental care
- saddling or harnessing (on and off)
- waiting (to pass through a gate or to begin an activity)
- commotion and/or other horses moving around
- hosing down
- mounting and dismounting (saddle or cart).

Once we've taught the horse to be confident about standing on a mat for longer and longer (*duration*), we can ask him to stay parked on a mat while we play with other exercises.

#6-#12 *HorseGym with Boots* (inclusive), look at ways of using mats in our training.

Duration means that we have carefully taught the horse to stay on a mat for increasing lengths of time. We start with one second and slowly work up to sixty seconds or more. *#8 HorseGym with Boots* shows how Boots and I worked this out.

When we first build duration on the mat, it's easier for the horse if we stay beside him, standing or sitting in a chair. However, we also want to be able to move around the horse while he stays confident and relaxed on a mat.

#15 HorseGym with Boots demonstrates how the handler can gradually increase his or her distance from the horse while maintaining the horse's confidence.

Once the horse is confident with staying on his mat for a good length of time, and is relaxed about the handler moving further away in different directions, we can work on building confidence with commotion such as:
- handler moves to stand in a relaxed manner at many points in a circle around the horse

- handler walks a brisk circle around the horse, both clockwise and anticlockwise
- handler jogs or runs around the horse both clockwise and anticlockwise
- handler jogs away from the horse and back again.

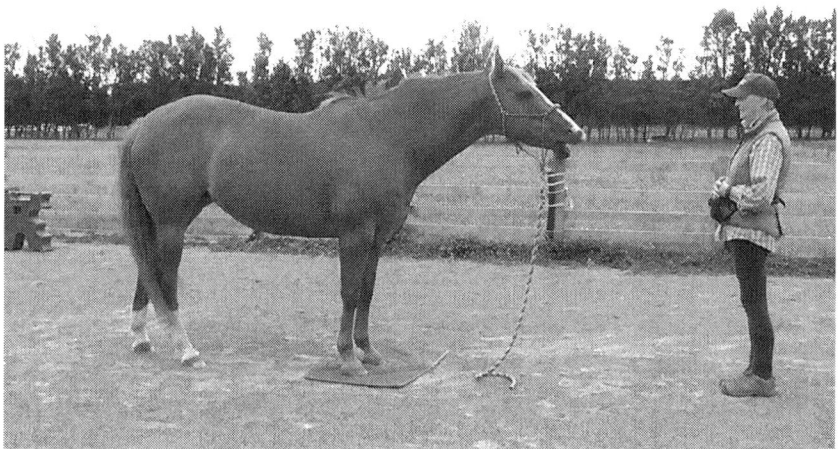

Figure 84: Boots is ground-tied at a mat. Bridget has walked a couple of steps away, turned and is waiting in a neutral body position. Note her hands set together, quietly resting on her belly button. We can gradually increase the distance away from the horse as well as gradually increasing how long we wait before returning to the horse to deliver the click&treat. Boots is trying her smile to see if she can get Bridget to click&treat by initiating an interaction.

Take Frequent Breaks

When we teach confident parking, it's important to take the horse for a walk away from the mat after a few minutes of parking practice, do something else, and then come back to it. If we lay out several mats, we can walk between them and do a bit of parking at each mat.

Many short segments of a specific task like this, with breaks to do other things we already know well, makes a session more interesting and gives the brain (the horse's and ours) more opportunity to build and strengthen nerve pathways for the new learning.

B. Using Mats as Destinations

On the mind map in Figure 83, there is a two-way arrow between the *Mat Destinations* and *Voice Signal* branches.

The two-way arrow is meaningful. If we use mats as destinations where the horse earns a click&treat each time he places his front feet on the mat, we have a ready-made halt behavior that we can use to teach our "Whoa" voice signal.

Training Plan Four in my book, *How to Begin Equine Clicker Training: Improve Horse-Human Communication*, looks in detail at how to get started with using a mat as a foot target.

If we always reinforce with relaxation (click&treat) when the horse puts his front feet on the mat, the horse soon sees the mat as a desirable stopping destination.

Then we can use mats to help the horse understand a variety of other things we would like him to learn.

C. Leading Willingly and a Nice Back Up

Loose-rope leading is covered in detail in my book, *Walking with Horses: The Eight Leading Positions*.

#27-#30 HorseGym with Boots (inclusive), outline ways of having fun teaching loose-rope leading while walking shoulder-to-shoulder. #27 also looks at teaching a nice back up.

If the horse confidently walks beside us and follows our body language for halting, backing up and turning on a loose lead, we have a strong basis for teaching ground-tying.

D. Teaching the "Whoa" Voice Signal

When the horse readily goes to a mat and halts with his front feet on it, we can use a distinct, consistent "Whoa" voice signal just as the horse is *bringing himself to a halt* at the mat. Lots of short frequent practices using a variety of mats in different places and situations will generalize the "Whoa" voice signal.

The "Whoa" voice signal is probably one of the most useful habits we can teach our horse, whether we are walking with him, driving or riding. If we always follow up his halt with a click&treat, we've helped the horse build a lovely habit without the use of physical pressure.

E. Rope Relaxation

Another prerequisite is something I've called *Rope Relaxation*. If we are going to drop the horse's lead rope on the ground, we first want the horse to understand all the strange things a rope might do.

There are several elements to Rope Relaxation. *#22 HorseGym with Boots* shows some of the elements mentioned in the list coming up.

#60 HorseGym with Boots is a more recent clip called *Rope Calmness* that shows some of the same elements plus a few others.

We want to gain the horse's confidence to remain parked while we do the following activities.
1. Swing a second rope (not attached to the horse) near him.
2. Toss the end of a rope all over his body, including around behind, under the belly and around the legs. Start with a second rope not attached to the horse, then graduate to using the end of a long lead rope.
3. When the rope is attached to the horse, make sure you keep a constant drape in the part attached to his halter while you toss the other end around his body. You want to avoid putting touch pressure on the halter.
4. Toss a coiled rope (not attached to the horse) in the air across him.
5. Randomly drop a coil of rope (not attached to the horse) onto the ground in various positions around him.

We want to continue building his confidence with the rope when we:
- drag a second rope while we walk along with the horse on a loose lead
- attach a second dragging rope to the horse's halter while we walk with him on a loose lead, including

walking curves and corners where the dragging rope may touch the horse's feet or legs.

Once we know the horse is cool about walking along with a dragging rope attached to his halter, we are ready to introduce ground-tying. No matter how carefully we try to control the environment, occasions will arise when something causes a ground-tied horse to move.

If we've carefully taught the horse all about dragging a rope attached to his halter, so it's part of his ho-hum repertoire, there is a good chance that he will not panic when the rope moves with him.

Figure 85: If something motivates our horse to move while he is ground-tied, it's good to know that he has the skill of holding his head sideways so he doesn't tread on the rope, as Boots is demonstrating here.

Ground-Tying Training Plan

Once the horse willingly,
- halts with his front feet on a mat and will stay there for whatever duration you have taught him
- leads with a light hand on a loose (draped) lead rope
- halts when you use your voice "Whoa" signal (and your body language)

- remains relaxed with a rope tossed all over his body and around his legs
- remains relaxed when a dragging rope attached to his halter chases him,

we can proceed to teach him about being ground-tied.

The pictures coming up highlight some of the features of the thin-sliced Training Plan that follows.

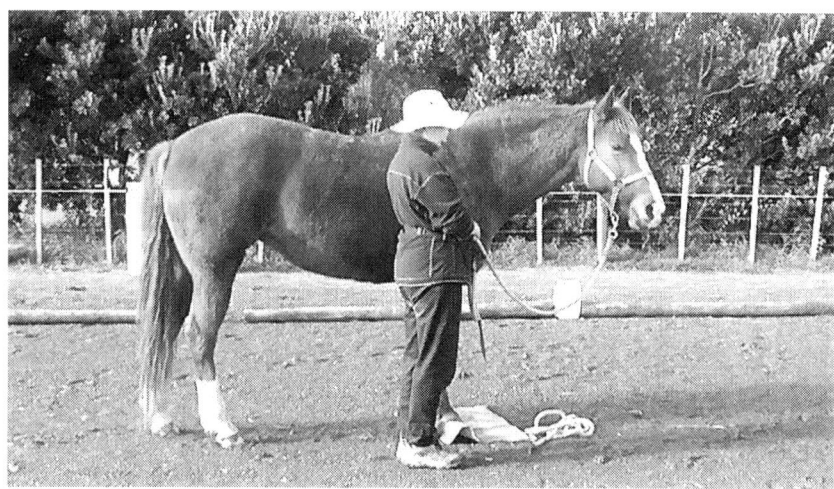

Figure 86: Boots and I have halted together at the mat. I've dropped a 2nd lead rope and am standing in my 'neutral' position (hands together on top of my belly button) as we build duration into the time that she stands quietly. Boots knows the task is finished when I click&treat. I am on her right side.

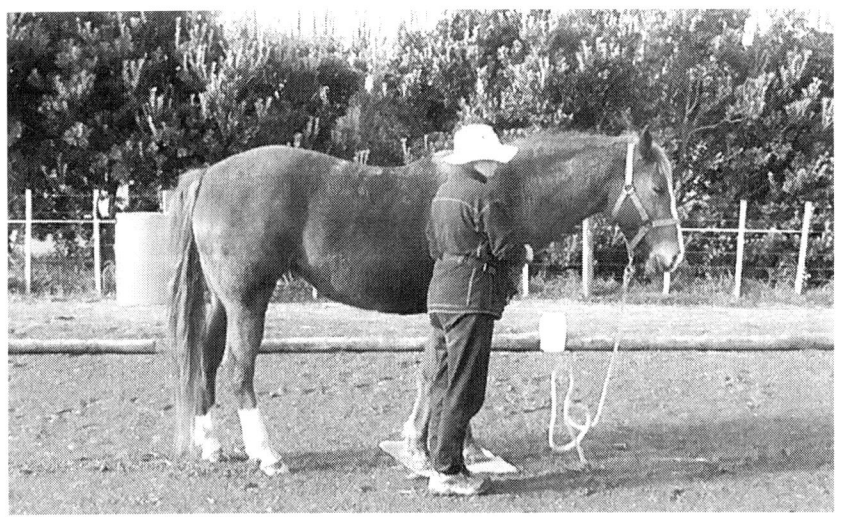

Figure 87: Now I'm dropping the actual lead rope. My next move is to take up a neutral 'waiting' body language position, before I relax (click&treat).

Figure 88: Boots and I halted together. I dropped the lead rope and I'm in the process of using a gesture signal as well as saying, "Wait," to let her know that I am going to walk on, but would like her to stay parked.

Figure 89: I've moved several steps away and I've turned to face Boots. Unless something very unusual happens, she will remain ground-tied until I walk back to her and reward her parking with a click&treat.

#72-73 *HorseGym with Boots* (inclusive) give an overview of this Training Plan.

In the chart coming up, the behavior of the handler is written first because the handler is initiating the action.

Chart of Possible Thin-Slices for the Ground-Tying Task

Slices (behavioral objectives)	Achieved
1. Walk on the horse's left side with a loose lead toward a mat: • halt with the horse at the mat using your "Whoa" voice signal and body language • drop a second rope (that you are carrying in your outside hand) on the ground under the horse's nose (see Figure 86). Allow him to satisfy his curiosity about it; relax (click&treat) • keep a 'smile' in your actual lead rope • pick up the dropped rope and walk together to the next mat or walk a large loop that returns you to the same mat.	

Horse halts with front feet on the mat and remains relaxed when the second rope is dropped and picked up again.

- ➤ If you set up a circuit of several mats, you can move smoothly from mat to mat.
- ➤ Remember to do something easy the horse already knows in between bursts of action on this new task.
- ➤ If you have a circuit of four or six mats, do the circuit once on each side of the horse, have fun doing something else that's easy, and come back to the circuit again if it feels right to do more.

2. As 1, but walking on the horse's right side.

3. As 1, but <u>without using mats</u>:
- walk on the horse's left side and, at intervals, ask him to "Whoa" using voice and body language signals
- at the same moment, drop the second rope that you are carrying under the horse's nose and let him satisfy any curiosity
- relax (click&treat) after you've dropped the rope
- everything stays the same except that we have removed the prop of the mat.

Horse halts and remains relaxed when you use your body language, your voice signal and drop the second rope.

- ➤ It may help the horse at first if you walk the same circuit as you walked when you were using the mats.
- ➤ Halt and drop the second rope where the mats were during the previous lesson.
- ➤ Once the horse seems to recognize the dropped rope as a place to stop and stand, gradually generalize to new areas.

4. As 3, but walking on the horse's right side.

5. As 3, but <u>drop the lead rope itself</u> (Figure 87):
   - walk on the horse's left side and at intervals, ask him to "Whoa" using body language and voice signals plus, at the same moment, drop the lead rope
   - relax as the horse halts; pause for a second or two, with neutral body language, to begin building duration into the time the horse stands quietly (see Figure 86)
   - click&treat well <u>before</u> the horse shows any tendency to move
   - everything stays the same except that we are dropping the lead rope rather than a second rope and waiting a moment before the click&treat.

Horse halts when you use body language and voice signal plus drop the lead rope and relax (click&treat). Horse relaxes too.

6. As 5, but walking on the horse's right side.
   - ➢ It's helpful if we can ground-tie the horse after asking him to back up.
   - ➢ For ground-tying, it's probably most handy to ask the horse to back up staying in the leading position beside his neck or shoulder. For more backing information, see *#27 HorseGym with Boots*.
   - ➢ Sometimes we may ask the horse to ground-tie after backing him up while we are face-to-face with him. It's always nice to have several ways of doing something. For more information about backing up face-to-face, see *#41 HorseGym with Boots*.

7. <u>Ask the horse to back up</u> positioned on his left side and while he is backing:

<ul><li>drop the lead rope and at the same time use your "Whoa" voice signal, relax (click&treat) when the horse halts</li><li>intersperse these with walking forward.</li></ul>	
Horse backs up on request and halts with the handler's voice "Whoa" signal plus the dropped rope.	
8. As 7, but positioned on the horse's right side.	
9. Experiment to see what happens when:<ul><li>walking on the horse's left side, you slow to a halt and gently drop the lead rope without using your voice "Whoa" signal as well</li><li>if you have developed clear body language to communicate that you are going to stop, the horse will respond to just your body language and the dropped rope</li><li>relax (click&treat) at the first sign of a halt</li><li>if the horse finds this difficult, leave it out for now and maybe return to it as part of your generalization when he knows the ground-tying task better.</li></ul>	
Horse brings himself to a halt when the handler halts and the rope is gently dropped in front of him in the absence of a voice "Whoa" signal.	
10. As 9, but walking on the horse's right side.	
11. Positioned on the horse's left side, ask him to jog (or trot) with you and halt with you when you halt. Use your voice signal plus drop the lead rope from the jog. When you begin trotting:<ul><li>you may find it helpful to use mats again until the halt from trot/jog is well established</li></ul>	

• maybe also begin with a second rope to drop rather than the lead rope.	

Horse willingly halts from jog/trot when the handler halts, gives the voice signal and drops the rope.

12. As 11, but jogging on the horse's right side.

Horse stops when rope is dropped & stays while handler walks away.
- ➢ Slices 1-12 above have the handler <u>stopping with the horse</u>.
- ➢ Now you want to make the task a bit more complex.
- ➢ You'll ask the horse to halt at a mat, drop the lead rope, and design a 'wait' signal to let the horse know you want him to remain parked while you move away from him (see Figure 88). For the 'wait' I like to use a gesture and a voice signal at the same time.
- ➢ For the early lessons, it is good to use a circuit of mats again, until you see that the horse understands the new nuances of the task consistently over several sessions.

13. Walk on the horse's left side with a loose lead toward a mat. Halt with horse at the mat using:
- "Whoa" voice signal
- dropped lead rope
- the voice and gesture 'wait' signals you have decided on

Then walk a few steps forward away from the horse.
- Turn and face the horse (see Figure 89) and take up a neutral body language position – placing both hands flat over your belly button (see Figure 86).

- Wait a second or two, be sure to return before the horse even thinks about moving. Count the seconds. Start with one second and don't wait longer until one second is completely okay with the horse.
- If the horse does move, gently return to him, pick up the lead rope, walk together in a relaxed manner and start again. Don't make the horse feel wrong. He can't be wrong because he doesn't yet know what you want. Next time return to him sooner rather than waiting that extra moment.
- Return to the horse; relax (click&treat).
- Pick up the lead rope and walk on to the next mat or walk a loop to return to the same mat.

Horse halts at mat and remains there confidently while the handler walks on a few steps, turns, pauses, and walks back to the horse.

14. As 13, but walking on the horse's right side.

15. Gradually walk a few more steps away from the horse and increase how long you wait before returning to the horse; relax (click&treat). Click&treat after you return to the horse.

If he loses confidence, immediately return to the distance and time he can cope with. Add distance and duration very slowly – one second and/or half a step at a time.

Horse stays with the mat and the dropped rope until the handler returns.

16. Make sure the horse is comfortable when you leave from his left eye and from his right eye. Spend a bit more time with the harder side, if there is one.

- ➤ The next slice asks the horse to halt at the mat while you keep on walking. You drop the lead rope and use your "Whoa" voice signal and your voice & gesture 'stay' signals but you don't halt yourself – you keep on walking.
- ➤ If the horse has been mainly watching your body language as his signal to halt, it could be hard for him at first until he realizes that,
  - the mat
  - dropped lead rope
  - voice signal,

  all mean he still should halt, even if you keep moving.

17. On the horse's *left* side, walk toward a mat with a loose lead. When you reach the mat, simultaneously:
    - use your "Whoa" voice signal
    - drop the lead rope
    - give your 'wait' signal without stopping your feet when the horse stops
    - walk on a few steps.

Turn and face the horse, then:
- wait a second or two
- return to the horse
- relax (click&treat)
- pick up the lead rope and walk on to the next mat.

Horse stays halted on the mat while the handler walks on, halts, turns, pauses and walks back to the horse.

18. As 17, but walking on the horse's right side.

19. Play with 17 and 18 gradually moving further away from the horse.

Horse stays parked at the mat while the handler moves away, pauses and returns to him.	
20. Play with 17 and 18 at the trot. Handler keeps jogging forward while the horse halts on the mat.	
Horse parks at the mat from the trot and stays parked while the handler jogs on, halts, turns, pauses and walks back to the horse.	
21. Play with 17 and 18 <u>without the mat</u> at the walk.	
Horse halts with voice and dropped rope and gesture signals and stays parked (no mat) while the handler walks on, turns, pauses and walks back to the horse.	
22. Play with 17 and 18 without the mat at a jog.	
Horse halts with voice and dropped rope signals and stays parked (no mat) while the handler jogs on, turns, pauses and jogs back to the horse.	

Generalization

Generalize ground-tying to new venues and around new distractions, as long as it's safe. Include the mat initially if it helps the horse, then phase it out.

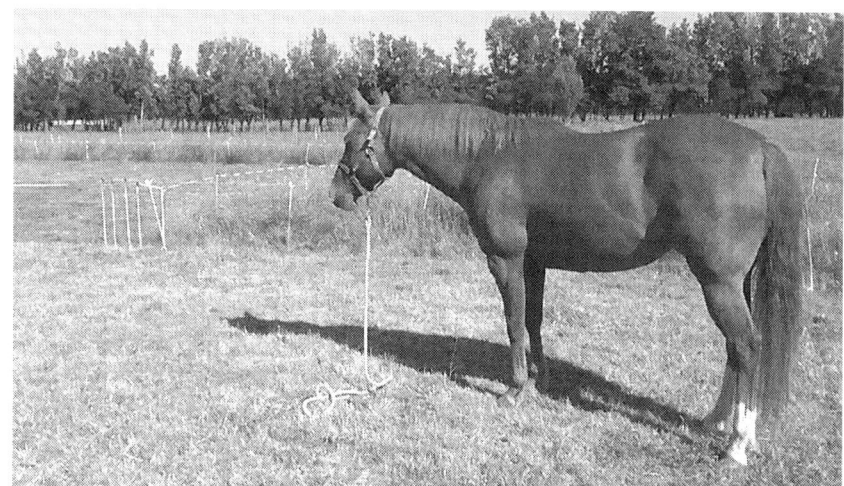

Figure 90: Once the horse is confident staying ground-tied in his familiar training area, generalize it to new situations and new venues.

If you are working on trailer-loading, generalize toward building the horse's confidence to stay parked when you go out of sight. Horses living naturally usually stay in visual contact with their band members. A horse suddenly left on his own feels vulnerable and usually becomes anxious.

If you've ever been out with another person and they suddenly disappear, you will know how this feels, especially if the other person is a toddler or you are in an unfamiliar place.

A horse may enter a trailer willingly, but become extremely worried when his handler (the herd member he is relying on) suddenly disappears from view. So teaching a horse that you may disappear, soon to reappear, is a useful pre-trailer-loading exercise.

#18 HorseGym with Boots demonstrates how I increased Boots' tolerance to my disappearance. You can see how quickly Boots becomes anxious when I move out of sight.

Short Summary of the Ground-Tying Training Plan

The numbers in the summary chart *do not* relate to the numbers in the previous detailed Training Plan chart. C&T = click&treat.

Summary of the Key Ground-tying Slices	Done
1. Halt together at a mat & drop 2nd rope, relax, wait, C&T.	
Horse halts with front feet on the mat and remains relaxed when the rope is dropped and picked up again.	
2. Without using mats, halt together and drop 2nd rope, relax, wait, C&T.	
Horse halts and remains relaxed when you give the "Whoa" voice signal and drop the rope	
3. Drop the lead rope itself instead of a spare 2nd rope, relax, wait, C&T.	
Horse halts and remains relaxed when you give the "Whoa" voice signal and drop the lead rope.	
4. Halt from a back-up, drop the rope, relax, wait, C&T.	
Horse backs up on request and halts with the handler's "Whoa" voice signal and the dropped rope.	
5. Experiment to see if the horse will halt with just the dropped rope signal and your body language (no voice signal).	
Horse brings himself to a halt when the rope is dropped in front of him in the absence of a "Whoa" voice signal.	
6. Halt together from a jog with body language, dropped rope, voice signal used simultaneously. (Maybe also use a mat at first.)	
Horse willingly halts from jog or trot.	
7. Experiment with dropping the rope before you use your voice signal.	
Horse begins to halt when he notes your body language and sees or feels the rope dropping.	

8. Halt with the horse <u>at a mat</u>, drop the rope, give a 'wait' signal and walk forward a few paces, turn, relax, pause, return to horse, C&T.	
Horse halts at the mat and remains there confidently.	
9. As 8 but walk further away, turn, relax, pause, return to horse, C&T.	
Horse stays with the mat and dropped rope until the handler returns.	
10. Handler drops the rope at the mat and keeps on walking without stopping first, turns, relaxes, pauses, returns to horse, C&T.	
Horse stays halted on the mat while the handler keeps walking.	
11. Play with 10 gradually moving further away from the horse, turn, relax, pause, return to horse, C&T.	
Horse remains confidently parked until the handler returns.	
12. Play with 10 <u>at the trot</u>. Handler keeps jogging forward after the horse halts on the mat.	
Horse parks from the trot and stays parked at the mat while the handler jogs on.	
13. Play with 10 <u>without the mat</u> at walk.	
Horse halts with voice and dropped rope signals (no mat) while handler walks on.	
14. Play with 10, without the mat, at a jog.	
Horse halts with voice and dropped rope signals (no mat) while handler jogs on.	
Generalize ground-tying to new venues and around new distractions. Include the mat initially if it helps the horse, then phase it out. Stay safe.	

Reminders

When we want to train something new, the first step is to scope the topic and define the specific task we want to focus on first. Once the specific task is decided, we can thin-slice it. We start by brainstorming everything related to the task that comes to mind.

Next, we arrange all the ideas from the brainstorm into an order that seems to make sense. We can always change our minds later.

Then it's time to gently experiment to see what we know already and what our horse can already offer in relation to the new goal we'd like to achieve.

This will give us an idea about where our Individual Education Program (IEP) needs to start. We want to base it on foundation training (and environmental situations) with which the horse is already confident or at least familiar.

Experimentation also helps us find any training holes that we need to fill before we enthusiastically head toward setting a new challenge for our horse.

Once we have written our thin-sliced Training Plan and found a starting point, we can begin to design our Individual Education Program by tailoring the thin-slices to suit our unique training environments, our knowledge as a handler, and the horse we are working with.

For example, Horse Agility occasionally has fun classes. One of them is to film our horse doing ten different tricks. A new trick for us was to ask Boots to step a foot on one end of a board set up as a seesaw to give a Teddy bear a seesaw ride. It's an exercise about how accurately and consistently she can place a single foot on request.

During our experimental stage, we found that previous tasks with rails and boards (straddling a rail, standing on a balance beam, putting all four feet on a small board, side-passing along a rail, backing over a rail) were firmly in her mind.

When I set out a long board about four inches wide, she naturally wondered which of the above I wanted her to do. Since it was none of them, we had a puzzle.

It was fun to break the task down so it made sense for Boots. Our Individual Education Program had the following behavioral objectives (slices). We played with it briefly most days for about five weeks, staying with each slice until she could do it confidently. A video clip of the process, called *Thin-Slicing the SeeSaw for Teddy* is in my *Thin-slicing Examples* playlist.

1. Step cleanly on a round white plastic lid with a front foot. She tended to paw at the lid and send it flying some of the time.
2. Tack a white lid to a small square of board so it has a one inch 'step up' factor like the seesaw board will have.
3. Tack a white lid to the end of the seesaw board. Hopefully she will focus on putting her foot on the white lid rather than try to maneuver her whole body onto the board.
4. Set the board on a fulcrum for the seesaw effect. This means that the end of the board, where she has to put her foot, is now off the ground.
5. Set up the board on a fulcrum with the Teddy bear mounted at one end.

Figure 91: Boots has worked out the puzzle about giving the Teddy a seesaw ride using her foot.

Chapter 9 finishes off the book with a summary about creating Training Plans and Individual Education Programs.

Careful front-end planning gives our training good direction and a giant motivational boost.

Chapter 9
Summary of the Planning Process

1. Decide on a Topic

Everything we do with our horse needs to be designed to increase his confidence in the human-dominated world he has to live in. If we are watching and listening, the horse will usually tell us what we should work on next.

Your topic could relate to:
- haltering
- leading
- everyday care
- grooming
- feeding time
- something specific like safety through gates
- teaching various leading positions
- hoof care
- vet procedures
- ground-work skills
- gymnastic exercises for general fitness
- rope relaxation and calmness
- wearing saddle or harness
- mounting blocks, mounting, dismounting
- riding or driving
- specifics for competitions
- tricks for fun
- walking or riding out alone
- walking or riding out with other horses
- staying parked at a target or ground-tied
- road and traffic confidence
- trail confidence
- recovery from injury
- rehabilitation from abuse

- specific skills such as cow work, Riding for the Disabled (RDA), police, cavalry, drum horses, parades
- public demonstrations.

This is not an exhaustive list, but many of the things we want to teach a horse would probably fit somewhere in one of the categories.

2. Scope the Topic and Seek the Prerequisites

Once you have determined your topic, take the time to mind map it or make a list of all the aspects of the topic that you can think of.

Probably you will come up with a set of individual tasks that all relate to your topic. You then have to decide which task to focus on first.

Prerequisites:

You may find that what seems like a simple task at first glance actually needs a whole series of prerequisite mini-skills to create a solid foundation on which the new task can be built.

People have a tendency to just go ahead and attempt to recreate something they have seen or heard. It's easy to rush in without much thought or reflection about what we are actually expecting the horse to know and do.

We can't expect a horse to be okay with a dragging rope unless we have quietly and carefully taught him confidence with ropes in a variety of situations.

We can't expect a horse to stand still willingly while we do things to him, unless we have quietly and carefully taught him that standing still without being tied up is okay.

Scoping your topic on paper goes hand in hand with mild experimentation with the horse to get a good idea of what the two of you can do already. Once you've experimented a bit, it's easier to decide what your first task should be.

If our final goal is complex, we achieve it by teaching a set of related tasks that are gradually chained together.

3. Define a Specific Task (ABCD)

You have scoped the topic and picked one aspect that you want to use as a task to teach the horse. You may want to eventually teach a whole series of things relating to your topic. A mind map of your topic makes it easy to organize a way to work through a series of tasks.

We can outline the decreasing complexity of what we are teaching like this:
- **topic**
  - **goals** within the topic
    - **tasks** to achieve a specific goal
      - **thin-slices** to achieve each task.

Thin-slices allow us to achieve a task. Several tasks allow us to achieve a goal. The goal is part of a larger training topic.

It's important to set tasks that you are able to achieve in a relatively short time frame. Some goals might be so small that they easily become one task.

On the other hand, a major goal may take months or years to achieve. But the tasks leading to that goal should be small enough so that the horse and the handler have continuous experiences of small achievements.

For example, your goal might ultimately be to ask your horse to jump a circuit of seven jumps, but if your horse is new to jumping, it pays to start with one jump and teach your signals really well. Your signals will then easily translate to two jumps in a row, three jumps and so on.

Not only would you start with one jump, you'd probably start with one rail on the ground. If you are teaching jumping as ground-work, a prerequisite would be that your horse walks and jogs beside you confidently with a loose lead rope.

If you are riding, your prerequisites will be good upward and downward transitions carried out calmly. If riding, you also have your own necessary personal prerequisites, such as a well-balanced independent seat on the horse, rising in your stirrups, light hands on the reins, and so on.

If the goal is to have your horse confidently jump seven jumps in a row as a ground-work gymnastic exercise, your first defined task would be to have him confidently going over one jump while you move beside him. You don't want him rushing toward it or accelerating with excitement after it. You want your movements and his movements to stay synchronized.

I won't pursue this example any further, but I think it gives you the idea. When Boots and I had a ground-work challenge called: *Jump a Course of Seven Obstacles*, it was an interesting learning curve for both of us because she is not a keen or natural jumper and I had to factor in my dodgy knees.

Also, at the time, I knew nothing about setting up jumps with exactly one, two or three strides between them. A short clip called *Jumping with Commentary* can be found in my *2015 Horse Agility* playlist.

Defining a specific task is made easier by using the **ABCD** method outlined in Chapter 6.

Audience: think of the horse's character type and what best motivates him. What do you think he may find easy or hard? If you are coaching another person, consider the character type of the person too. If you are working by yourself, consider your own character type.

Behavior: exactly what do you want to see when the horse is carrying out the task the way you want? Sometimes as well as seeing, we can feel the horse's response through the rope or reins, or we feel his body energy. Additionally, how do you want your signals for the horse to look and feel?

Conditions: in what venue, with what props, in what environment, with or without head gear, rope, reins or neck rope?

Degree of Perfection or Proficiency: how are you going to measure what you are doing? Decide on how long, how many strides, how many rails, how many jumps, zero tight lead-ropes, how far, how fast? Once you have taught the basic task, you can develop it so it is performed more proficiently or at a higher standard.

When you describe a task with these **ABCD** points in place, your Training Plan will progress nicely. Not defining a task clearly is a major hurdle to good planning and good training outcomes.

4. Venues, Props and Time

Write down possible training venues, time you have available, time it may take the horse to learn the task, props and helpers you have available.

You outlined the **conditions** for teaching when you defined your task. Now is the time to work out the detail of where and when and how you can ensure the conditions that will make the teaching and learning as easy as possible.

This is especially important if you have to book venues or check when your helper might be available.

5. Brainstorm Possible Thin-Slices

Now all your thinking about your defined task is put to work to create a brainstorm or mind map of the smallest parts (slices) that make up the overall task. (See Figures 73 and 83.)

Remember, it's easy to have too few slices, but we can never have too many. The more we can keep the horse feeling successful, the more he will enjoy his sessions.

6. Slices in an Order that Might Work = Training Plan

Once you have a brainstormed list, or a mind map of the smallest slices you can think of, it's time to put them into an order that might work nicely for you and the horse.

As always, you can add, delete or move your ideas around. If we've thought through the slices on paper, it's easier to work with them when we're out with the horse. Pocket cue cards with the slices listed in order can be helpful. I generally use these if I'm working on a complex task.

When you've completed this step, your Training Plan is done!

7. Decide How You Will Document Your Progress

Before you move from your Training Plan into your Individual Education Program, decide how you will keep a record of what you're doing, when you did it and how it went during each session.

The last part of Chapter 4 looked at a variety of examples for record-keeping (in the *Horse Folder* section).

8. Experiment to Find a Starting Point

By experimenting with yourself and the horse, you can find out whether your thin-slices are thin enough and whether you have thought through the prerequisites carefully enough. You want to begin the task at a point where both you and the horse are relaxed and confident.

You can, of course, do gentle experimentation any time during the planning process. If you mostly work with the same horse, your starting points may become obvious while you are doing other things.

9. Outline your Individual Education Program

Now is the time to tailor your Training Plan by taking into account the character type, health, age, fitness level and background experience of your horse and yourself. You already considered this to some extent when you thought about the **A**udience portion of the **ABCD** used for defining your task.

Your experimentation may show that your Training Plan was too ambitious and you need to slow down and do more thin-slicing of certain parts. Or you may discover that the horse knows more than you realized, so you can drop some of the foundation lessons from the IEP.

You may discover that your horse finds something particularly difficult, so you give that more time and attention. Life, weather or injury may interfere, forcing you to adjust the time frame.

You may decide your defined task was too large, so you go back to redefine it until it feels like a task you can master in a comfortable, shorter time frame. As mentioned earlier, it's important that the tasks you set are achievable in a relatively short time frame. Each small success is worth its weight in gold for motivation to keep learning.

10. Tweak Your IEP

Each session with your horse gives you valuable feedback and new ideas. Things that *don't* work are just as valuable as things that *do* work. By working with a pre-planned set of thin-slices, we can avoid a lot of unfocused activity that confuses the horse and leads to handler frustration.

Inevitably, we'll still get occasional confusion. The IEP is always a work in progress. Tweak it as you get new information by listening to your horse and when you make new connections as you think through a challenge.

Conclusion

It's my hope that this book has given you a few ideas to make your training sessions fun for all concerned. Horses love clarity. If they can understand what we would like them to do, most horses comply willingly.

If we take the time and make the effort to:
- define our tasks carefully
- thin-slice the procedure into a Training Plan
- write IEPs for individual horses and ourselves or the horse's handler
- listen carefully for feedback so we can tweak our program to make it better,

we're doing our best to give the horse a good deal.

Appendix 1: Starting Clicker Training

Materials: Gear Checklist

1. A **training venue** where the horse feels comfortable. Ideally, his herd buddies are in view but not able to interfere.
2. The horse behind a **safe barrier**. This could be a non-wire fence or a gate or stall guard.

Figure 1: When starting a horse off with clicker training, it's wise to use protected contact, which just means keeping a barrier between you and the horse until you have established good table manners. Sometimes your only safe option might be to tie the horse up as in Figure 2. Protected contact allows you to step out of reach if the horse becomes over-enthusiastic.

Figure 2: Sometimes our only safe option is to have the horse tied up. Tying up with a wide halter is safer than tying with a rope halter in case something causes the horse to pull back. We're also using a Blocker Tie Ring. If the horse pulls back, there will be friction on the rope, but the rope can pull free completely, so the horse's whole weight won't be impacting the sensitive neck vertebrae.

You can find out more about the Blocker tie ring at: http://blockerranch.com/.

If the horse is tied up, make sure that he is able to relax when he is tied and that you allow him enough rope so he can easily engage with the target.

Protected contact allows you to stay safe if the horse becomes overly keen or excited about the idea of earning a tasty treat. You won't know how he will react until you try it out.

3. Decide on your **marker sound**; organize your mechanical clicker if you intend to use one. Having it on a cord around your neck or wrist means you can let go of it when you need to use your hand. But it also means you have to get it ready before you want to use it again so the timing of your click is accurate. I use a mechanical clicker sometimes to teach something new, but most of the time I use a tongue click. If you can't make a clear

tongue click sound, a special short, sharp word or sound (not used any other time) works just as well. For simplicity in these notes, I'll use the word 'click' to refer to whatever marker sound you decide to use.

4. You need a **pouch or pocket** that easily lets your hand to slip in and out. One of my favorites is a hoodie-style sweatshirt with a continuous front pocket that allows me easy access to the treats with either hand. Mostly I use a bum bag (fanny pack) type pouch.

5. The **treats**: people use tiny portions of carrot, apple, celery, grain, horse nuts, cereal, crackers, dry bread, popped popcorn — anything your horse likes. Individual pieces are often easier to manage than loose grain. Casual experimentation lets you find out which treats your horse likes best. My horse loves peppermints, so we use these for very special occasions like a superb response when we are learning something new. Often I have a variety of treats. Apple pieces score higher with my horse than carrot pieces.

Figure 3: It doesn't take long to get into the habit of getting the treats ready before heading out our horse.

6. You can **count out a specific number of treats** for a short training session or just have an abundant treat supply at hand. Running out of treats during a session is not a nice feel for the horse. I usually have spare horse pellets handy in a sealed container in case I need more.
7. You need a **hand-held target** to teach the horse that he has to *physically do something* (e.g. touch his nose to the target) in order to earn the click&treat. It's easiest to start with a target on a stick. A plastic drink bottle taped to a stick makes a nice safe, lightweight target. If the horse is nervous of sticks due to past experiences, a plastic bottle by itself, as in Figure 4 may be a better way to start. Some people use a fly swatter.
8. Ensure that the horse is **not hungry**. We want the horse to be interested, but not over-excited by the idea of special food coming his way.
9. If your horse is on restricted calories, ensure that his treats are counted as part of his daily total.

Two Extra Points

1. If the horse is wary about a new object like a target on a stick or a plastic bottle, I like to walk away backwards with the object (or have a helper walk away backwards with it while the horse and I follow together), and encourage the horse to follow until he makes up his own mind that it is okay to put his nose near or on the new item. Horses tend to follow things moving away and retreat from things moving toward them.
2. If you click by mistake, it's best to deliver the treat anyway. At this point you are training to give meaning to the click, so this is important. We want *the click and the treat* to belong together in the horse's mind.

Method

1. Simulation: Giving Meaning to the Click

It's ideal to learn the process of giving meaning to the click with a person standing in for the horse. The more adept we are with the mechanics of treat delivery before heading out to the horse, the more our horse will buy into our confidence that we know what we are doing.

1. Have your hand ready on the clicker (if using a clicker).
2. Present the target a little bit away from the person, so he or she has to reach toward it to touch it.

Figure 4: Learning the mechanics of the process with another person standing in for the horse means that the horse doesn't have to put up with our first fumbling as we work it all out. We have to get our head and our muscle memory around how to carry out the routine smoothly. If we approach the horse confident with what we are doing, the horse will buy into our confidence.

3. *Wait* for the person to touch the target with their hand (be patient).
4. The instant they touch it, click or say your chosen word or sound.
5. Lower the target down and behind your body to take it out of play.
6. Reach into your pocket/pouch for the treat (maybe use coins or bits of cardboard or mini chocolates).
7. Extend your arm fully to deliver the treat.
8. Stretch your treat hand out flat so it is like a dinner plate with the treat on it.
9. Hold your arm and hand firm so your pretend horse can't push it down.
10. When the 'horse' has taken the treat, pause briefly, then begin again with #1.
11. *Ignore* any unwanted behavior as much as possible.
12. Turn a shoulder or move your body/pouch out of reach if the person pretending to be your horse tries to mug you for a treat. Your 'pretend horse' has to learn that he or she earns the click&treat only by touching the target. If your 'pretend horse' is strongly invasive, put a barrier between you.
13. Multiple short sessions (up to 3 minutes long) at different times allow your brain and your muscle memory to absorb the technique, especially the finer points of timing.
14. If your helper is willing, let him or her be the teacher and you take a turn being the horse. Playing with being the horse is often a real eye-opener.

2. With the Horse

A: Giving Meaning to the Click: Touching a Target

The final goal is for the horse to move willingly to follow the target so he can put his nose on it to earn a click&treat.

First Session

1. Count about 20 treats into your pocket/pouch. Have a few spares handy in case you want to finish the session by putting a handful of treats into the horse's food bucket as an *end of session* signal.

2. Hold the target near his nose, but don't *thrust* it at him.

3. *Wait* until he touches even a whisker to it - *click* and *move the target* out of sight behind you. Moving the target out of sight will encourage his attention to the target when you present it again for the next repeat.

4. As you move the target behind you, simultaneously *reach for the treat* and deliver it away from your body by holding your hand out straight and rotating your shoulder to create a solid platform with your totally flat hand.

Figure 5: Deliver the treat with a flat hand and an outstretched arm so your body is well away from the horse. After the click, I move the target out of sight behind me to 'take it out of play'. It will then be obvious to the horse when I present it again.

5. If using a mechanical clicker, put your hand on the clicker ready to click.

6. Then hold out the target again. In your early sessions, put the target in the same place so you keep it easy for the horse to touch. At some point you will see that he really *gets* the connection between touching the target, the click, and the treat.

7. Repeat until you've used up your 20 treats. Ignore unwanted behavior. Stop after a good response. A few treats in a feed dish or on the grass is a nice way to let the horse know that one of your mini-sessions is finished. Put the target away out of sight.

8. Lots of short sessions (about 20 treats or 3 minutes) work well. You can do other things with the horse between the mini clicker training sessions.

9. Keep all your 'targeting criteria' the same until you get 10/10 confident repeats in a row, every time, over at least three consecutive sessions.

   By targeting criteria, I mean:
   - where you train
   - where you stand in relation to the horse
   - how and where you present the target.

Create a consistent end of session game that lets the horse know that the clicker training session is about to finish. Boots likes to finish with a series of belly crunches or touching various body parts to my hand. When I actually stop, I use a voice signal, "All gone," along with a gesture made by swinging my arms back and forth across each other at waist level several times. A handful of treats in a food bowl or on the grass is one way to signal that we're finished for now. To find out more about belly crunches, check out www.Intrinzen.horse.

Part B coming up shortly outlines how to make the target more interesting once the horse is totally ho-hum and consistent with touching his nose to the target when you hold it out near his nose.

The clip called *Clicker 1 with Smoky* in my 'Starting Clicker Training' playlist illustrates the process of teaching the horse the connection between touching the target, the click, and the treat.

The method shown on the clip can be improved by not waiting so long to click&treat again. At first, it's good to click&treat often while the horse remains facing forward. In some parts of the clip we waited for Smoky to turn toward us and then turn away again before we clicked. That runs the risk of having the horse think that turning toward us first is part of what we want him to do.

B. Lunging for the Treat

Some horses are always polite, others not so.
1. Be safe. Put a barrier between you and the horse so you can move back out of range.
2. Make sure that the horse is **not hungry**. We want the horse interested in clicker work, but not over-excited or aroused by the thought of food treats.
3. Check out your **food delivery** method.
    a) Does it take too long to get your hand into and out of your pocket or pouch? Can you find easier pockets or a more open pouch?
    b) Do you move your hand toward your treats *before* you've clicked? This can cause major problems because the horse will be watching your hand rather than focusing on what you are teaching.
4. Be sure to only feed treats if they have been earned <u>and you have clicked</u>. Ask the horse to do something before giving a treat, either have him touch the target or take a step or two backwards.
5. Avoid feeding any treats by hand unless you have asked for a behavior and clicked for it. When not clicker training, put treats in a feed dish or on the grass.
6. Hold your treat hand where you want the horse to be rather than where he has stuck his nose. In the beginning, we want him to have his head straight to retrieve the treat. If he is over-eager, it can help to hold the treat toward his chest so he has to shift backwards to receive it.
7. If he lunges at your treat hand, take hold of the side of his halter after the click, so you have some control of where he puts his mouth. I also use a loud sharp, "Uh" (as in 'up') sound as a warning that the shark-like behavior is not what I'm after.

8. It can help to run your closed treat hand down the horse's nose from above, and ask him to target your fist before you open your hand so he can retrieve the treat.
9. It may also work to bring your fist (closed around the treat) up under his chin and have him target your fist before you flatten your hand so he can retrieve the treat. Often one of these little intervening steps can help build the habit of polite treat-taking.
10. A bit of experimentation will show you what works best with a particular horse.
11. With consistency and patience on the handler's part, over-enthusiastic treat-taking usually improves once the horse understands that a click&treat only follows when he carries out a request you have made. He'll learn that a treat will only follow if there has been a click first. That is why we have to be consistent.
12. The horse's character type will influence how he takes the treat.
13. Prompt, cleanly executed treat delivery is always important. Sloppy treat delivery is the first thing to look at if things are not going smoothly.

The clip called *Table Manners for Clicker Training* in my *Starting Clicker Training* playlist illustrates how we can use the timing of the click to improve the politeness around treat-retrieval. The clip shows Smoky early in his clicker training education and Zoe who had never done it before.

C: Targeting: next sessions

#2 HorseGym with Boots shows the process in action. I would improve the technique shown in the clip by withdrawing the target down behind me, rather than over my shoulder, and standing rather than sitting. Also, not all horses are comfortable working across electric fencing, even if it is not electrified.

1. Once the horse is confidently touching the target held near his nose and seldom loses focus, gradually change the position of the target to make it more challenging for him. Chose one of: higher, lower, to the right, to the left. Teach him each of these one at a time. Each change you make is a big deal for the horse.

2. When he moves his neck to follow the target willingly and with interest, ask him to move a step to the right or the left to reach it. Stay with one direction until he is superb at it, then teach the other direction.

3. When he happily moves one step, gradually build up more steps. You can still be on the other side of a barrier while you teach this.

5. Whenever you change a criterion, begin by clicking for even the smallest hint of behavior heading in the new direction, until the horse shows confidence with the change. Then start withholding the click to gradually get more of what you want.

6. If he gets confused, *always be ready to backtrack* to the place where he can be continuously successful. This is the key to overall success and rapid progress. If he gives up because it's too hard, you have lost his willingness.

7. Stop each session on a high. Horses think about these things overnight. Stopping on a good note helps his motivation to do it again next time. Our tendency is to see if the horse can do it again right away, so we have to remind ourselves to stop right after the best response.

8. When you feel safe, work without the barrier.

9. Get creative to see where he'll happily follow the target (toward, over, between, into and around things).

D. Destination Training

Once the horse understands nose targets, we can hang them around our training area and use them to teach the wonderful habits of a willing 'walk on' and a prompt 'halt'. It operates equally well with ground-work or riding.

Each target becomes a destination that the horse understands. Walking between destinations becomes interesting for the horse because there is always a positive consequence (click&treat) upon reaching the next target.

A clicker-savvy horse soon appreciates the fact that we know the way to the next destination that will earn him a pause and a click&treat. It gives him a reason to want to go where we want to go.

If a horse is barn- or buddy-sweet, we can put out targets to gradually build confidence with moving a bit further away. At some point, the horse's thoughts will be more on seeking out the next target than on his buddies, barn or paddock left behind.

It may seem like a lot of effort at first, but once we have gained the horse's confidence about willingly going out and about with us, we can gradually reduce and then phase out the target props. We can use environmental markers (trees, corners, nice grazing spots) instead.

#3 - #5 HorseGym with Boots (inclusive) demonstrate ways of using nose targets in different contexts.

As well as nose targets, we can teach the horse about foot targets using small boards or mats or something like a Frisbee. We can use these as parking spots.

#6 - #18 HorseGym with Boots (inclusive) deal mainly with foot targets.

Figure 7: Boots is parked on a mat while Bridget models various positions in relation to the horse. The various positions are the subject of my book, 'Walking with Horses'.

We can set out mats as destinations or we can use something like a Frisbee to toss ahead of us, move forward to target it, toss it again, and so on. It's another way we can teach him confidence about leaving his home area. We create an activity that gives him something positive to do.

Providing destinations for my horses was a real breakthrough in how fast they learned and how willingly they applied themselves to learning new tasks that required moving from point A to point B.

Conclusion

For people who have never explored equine clicker training, using a nose target is a great way to start because when you no longer want to do it, you simply put the target away.

Once you get in the habit of having treats with you, and your horse becomes clicker savvy, you may be tempted to use the mark and reward clicker training system to teach your horse other new things or to refine tasks that the horse already knows.

Working for a food reward (even such tiny ones) activates one of the most powerful seeking systems in the deepest part of the brain.

Of course, horses learn readily by seeking out what will *release* signal pressure, i.e. the discomfort-comfort dynamic. But the motivating factor of a food *reward* allows us to add a whole new dimension to our training. The horse can become proactive in his communication with us. It's also a lot more fun to work with.

Once they are clicker savvy, horses show a strong desire to work for a food reward. They love the click&treat dynamic because the click (or special word/sound) can be timed to tell them exactly what they did that will earn the treat. Horses love clarity. They like to be right in the same way as we like to be right.

The mark and reward (clicker training) system removes much of the guess-work the horse is faced with when we use only the release reinforcement system.

Most horse-human dysfunction is due to lack of clarity coming from the human side of the relationship for these reasons.

1. Our behavior around the horse is inconsistent.
2. Our signals to ask the horse to do something are inconsistent and/or poorly taught.
3. We are not able to read the horse's body language well enough to understand what he is saying to us.

Most horses are happy to comply with our requests if we teach what we want carefully and ensure our signals are clear and consistent.

Clicker training has the handler looking for the moments to reward, rather than moments that need correction. As the handler gets better and better at thin-slicing a large task into its smallest teachable parts, it becomes easier and easier for the horse to learn by being continually successful.

We learn to reset a task rather than correct something that did not go as we hoped. This makes a huge difference to how horses perceive their training. Clicker-savvy horses often don't want their sessions to end. The positive vibrations that go with good clicker training make it fun rather than a chore.

As mentioned earlier, equine clicker training gives us a way to let the horse know instantly, by the sound of the marker signal (click), when he is right. It takes away much of the guessing horses have to do as they strive to read our intent.

A great deal more detail is available in my book, *How to Begin Equine Clicker Training: Improve Horse-Human Communication.* It is available via Amazon.com as an e-book or a hard copy book.

Appendix 2
Stages of Learning
Acquisition, Fluidity, Generalization and Maintenance
Acquisition

Acquisition includes getting our head around how we will teach a new behavior and then explain it to the horse.

The way we first present new material to the horse is crucial. As much as possible, we want the horse to be continuously successful.

It's helpful to practice our ideas and techniques first on a person standing in for the horse. If you are lucky enough to have an experienced horse, it also helps to work out techniques with him before moving on to a novice horse.

Even a well-educated, experienced horse appreciates learning new things in small slices. This allows him to build confidence and expertise with each step toward being able to carry out the whole task smoothly.

It always pays to begin with low-key experimentation to see what the horse is already able to offer. We may find that some of the basic elements in our Individual Education Program (IEP) are missing or not quite good enough. We might find some major training holes that need to be addressed.

For example, before we can teach our horse to weave a series of objects, have we taught him to confidently walk with us on a loose lead rope? Does he easily stay beside us, stepping off when we step off, halting when we halt and turning when we turn?

Gentle experimentation may also lead us to discover that the horse already has a solid foundation on which we can easily build the new task.

Fluency

Once we have created an Individual Education Program and carefully taken the horse through it, we have acquired the ability to carry out a new behavior together.

If the task is part of daily general care and recreation, such as safe behavior around gates, the horse will have ample opportunity to use the new behavior often and receive reinforcement for it. His response to the signal will continue to become more fluent.

If, on the other hand, the new behavior is for a specific purpose, such as loading onto a trailer or trotting through a tunnel for Horse Agility, we have to set up special training opportunities to allow the horse to become fluent.

In my experience, if we train a new behavior to the point of fluency, the horse tends to remember it forever. If a behavior is unreliable, it was not originally taught to the point of fluency.

After my horse became fluent in navigating an S-bend of rails on the ground, I did not have to teach that obstacle again every time it was part of a Horse Agility course.

Figure 1: Fluency: For daily routines like moving through gates, fluency builds up quickly if our signals are clear and consistent. In this photo, the lead rope is tight. Ideally, we like the horse to move through the gate with a loose lead rather than rush through to grab a mouthful of fresh grass.

Figure 2: Fluency: Popping balloons is not something we do every day. For Boots to become fluent with balloon popping, I had to set up special sessions often enough for her to become confident and proficient.

Generalization

Once the horse understands a new task or a new skill, it is important to take it out into the world. That is what I mean by generalization. Through generalization, the horse gains further fluency with a task.

Generalization includes things like:
1. asking for the behavior in different places but still at home
2. using different props
3. working at different times of the day
4. working with a different handler (who uses the same signals)
5. asking for the behavior away from home
6. working with unusual distractions
7. working at a different gait
8. handler uses a different body orientation
9. fading out a signal and replacing it with a new one
10. if we are using clicker training, moving to occasional click&treat once the horse knows the task, rather than each time we ask for the behavior.

Figure 3: Generalization: Once our work at home on a loose lead is smooth, we can take our skills out on the road.

Generalization helps the horse put the new learning into his long-term memory. Each time we quietly repeat the task, we help build the horse's confidence. If the horse is unable to do the task in a specific situation, it gives us a clue about where we are in our Education Program with this horse, for this task.

Maintenance

As already mentioned under 'Fluency', some behaviors become and remain fluent because we use them a lot, for example, putting on and taking off a halter or cleaning out the feet every day.

Other behaviors are specialized and we have to create a plan to refresh and use them occasionally so that they stay in our repertoire. Vet procedures usually come into this category.

If we teach our horse to flex his neck toward the prick of a toothpick, so his muscles are loose rather than tight, we need to do this needle simulation on a regular basis. Likewise, if we want the horse to be confident with worming paste, we can practice with applesauce as frequently as we like.

Hoof trimming, whether we do it ourselves or hire someone, can cause anxiety for a horse if it suddenly happens out of the blue. It's much easier for us and the horse if we pick his feet up often. We can practice moving his feet into trimming positions, making it a regular request. We can also introduce the horse to a variety of different people who are allowed to touch him.

A list of the sorts of behaviors we would like our horse to maintain is a useful addition to our Horse Folder and can be fixed to the wall of our tack room.

Figure 4: Maintenance of a behaviour: Frequent picking up of feet and cleaning them out will help maintain confidence with prolonged foot handling when trimming time comes around.

Appendix 3: List of YouTube Video Clips

Most of the video clips are shorter than five minutes, so they are quick to watch and easy to review if you are interested in specific tasks.

> To reach my channel, put *Hertha MuddyHorse* into the YouTube search engine. The Clips are in one of three playlists.
>
> 1. Most of the clips are in my *HorseGym with Boots* playlist. Each title is written as *#? HorseGym with Boots*. For example, if you want to quickly find Clip number 22, simply put: *#22 HorseGym with Boots* into the YouTube search engine and it should come right up.
> 2. Some clips are in the *Free-Shaping Examples* playlist. These are named only, so to find a particular clip, go to that playlist and scroll down for the clip's name.
> 3. Other clips are in the *Thin-Slicing Examples* playlist. These are also only named, so you search the playlist for the title you want.

A list of all the current *HorseGym with Boots* Clips follows, as well as titles in the *Free-Shaping* and *Thin-Slicing* examples.

HorseGym with Boots Series

Topics are added to this series as they are created.
 1. Introduction
 2. Giving meaning to the click
 3. Stationary nose targets
 4. Parking at a nose target (also spooky new things to touch)

5. Putting behavior 'on cue'
6. Foot targets (also, free-shaping new behavior)
7. Backing up from the mat
8. Duration on the mat
9. Putting the mat target 'on cue'
10. Generalizing mats
11. Mat-a-thons
12. Chaining tasks
13. Anthem is new to nose targets (Anthem is a young quarter-horse)
14. Anthem is new to foot targets
15. Parking at a distance
16. The 'triple treat'
17. 'Walk-on' and 'halt' multi-cues
18. Parking out of sight
19. Free-shaping
20. The 'art of standing still'
21. Walk away for confidence (with new things)
22. Rope relaxation
23. Hosing on the mat (recognizing 'click points')
24. Parking commotions
25. Parking with ball commotion
26. *8 Leading Positions* overview
27. Good Backing = Good Leading
28. Leading Position Three (beside neck or shoulder)
29. Leading Position Three with a 'circle of markers'
30. Leading Position Three duration exercise
31. Natural and Educated body language signals
32. Sensitivity to Body language
33. Opportunity, Signals 1
34. Signals 2: Gestures
35. Signals 3: Touch
36. Signals 4: Verbal signals (also environmental signals, horse initiated signals and marker signals)
37. Signals 5: Intent
38. Signals 6: Body Orientation (of handler)
39. Train with a Lane 1
40. Train with a Lane 2

41. Leading Position Seven Clip 1 of 4, in front facing horse
42. Leading Position Seven Clip 2 of 4
43. Leading Position Seven Clip 3 of 4
44. Leading Position Seven Clip 4 of 4
45. Leading Position One: Clip 1 of 2 in front, facing away
46. Leading Position One Clip 2 of 2
47. Leading Position Two (horse's nose stays behind handler's shoulder)
48. Leading Position Eight Clip 1 of 7, Go, Whoa & Back (facing the horse's side)
49. Leading Position Eight Clip 2 of 7, Groom, Saddle, Relax
50. Leading Position Eight Clip 3 of 7, Drive-by Grooming & Mounting Prep
51. Leading Position Eight Clip 4 of 7, Side Step in Motion
52. Leading Position Eight Clip 5 of 7, Yielding Front End & Hind End
53. Leading Position Eight Clip 6 of 7, Side Step from Halt
54. Leading Position Eight Clip 7 of 7, Arc Exercise
55. Leading Positions Four and Five (beside ribs & beside butt)
56. Leading Position Four, Clip 2
57. Leading Position Six Clip 1 of 8, Liberty (behind horse)
58. Leading Position Six Clip 2 of 8, One long rein
59. Leading Position Six Clip 3 of 8, Square of lanes
60. Leading Position Six Clip 4 of 8, Rope Calmness
61. Leading Position Six Clip 5 of 8, Two Long Reins: Circle & Weaving
62. Leading Position Six Clip 6 of 8, 4 Leaf Clover Exercise
63. Leading Position Six Clip 7 of 8, 'Gates', Guided Rein, Obstacles
64. Leading Position Six Clip 8 of 8, Trailer Prep
65. Haltering process (with guided free-shaping)
66. Importance of Clear Signals

67. Prep 1 for Weaving, 90 and 180 degree turns; 'Draw' and 'Drive'
68. Weave Prep 2, 360 degree turns
69. Weave Prep 3, Weave a series of objects
70. Weave Prep 4, Only the horse weaves
71. Weave Prep 5, Curves, Circles, at Liberty
72. Ground-tie Clip 1, Getting Started
73. Ground-tie Clip 2, Another Venue
74. Thin-slicing a Trailer Simulation
75. Quiet Sharing of Time and Place
76. Active Sharing of Time and Place + Greet & Go
77. Claim the Spot
78. Watchfulness First Action
79. Watchfulness Second & Third Actions
80. Guiding from Behind
81. Shadow Me
82. Boomerang Frolic
83. Shadow Me Duration with Clicker Training
84. Shadow Me Using Targets

Thin-Slicing Examples

This playlist includes thin-slicing examples about the following topics. To find a specific clip, go to the *Thin-Slicing Examples* playlist in my channel and scroll down to find the one you want. New clips are added as they are made.

- Tunnel with Boots
- Pool Noodle task
- Head Rocking for Poll Relaxation
- Bottle Bank obstacle
- Zigzag for Horse Agility
- Yield Shoulder into a Turn on the Haunches
- Stepping over rails
- Soft yield to Rein Signals (5 Clips which also have their own Playlist)
- Thin-slice *'The Box'* Movement (back, sideways, forward, sideways)

- Backing up
- Rope Texting
- Thin-slicing the 1m board
- Water & Tarp obstacle
- Thin-slice the 'Shadow Me' Game at Liberty
- Free-shape Learning to Ring a Bell

Free-Shaping Examples

This playlist includes clips using the free-shaping technique to teach a task. To find a particular clip, go to the *Free-Shaping Examples* playlist in my channel and scroll down to find the clip you want. Most of these clips show both free-shaping and thin-slicing.
- Table Manners for Clicker Training
- Boots and Bicycle
- Bob meets Bicycle (Bob is a young quarter horse)
- Introduction to a saddle (with Bob, his first meeting with a saddle)
- Head-lowering (2 Clips)
- Clicker 1 with Smoky
- Smoky and Dumb-bell target
- Boots picks up the Dumb-bell
- Free-shape Learning to Ring a Bell

There are also short playlists on specific topics including:
- Thin-slicing the Wagon-wheel obstacle
- Teaching the S-bend
- Soft Yield to Rein Signals (5 clips)
- Hula Hoop Challenges (5 clips)
- Single Obstacle Challenges
- 2012 Horse Agility
- 2014 Horse Agility
- 2015 Horse Agility
- 2016 Horse Agility

Most of the Horse Agility clips have a commentary explaining the tasks and showing where we lost marks. Each task is marked out of ten, five points for the handler and five points for the horse. Some are at liberty and others are with halter and lead.

Reference List

Abrantes, Roger. DVDs (2013). *The 20 Principles all Animal Trainers Must Know.* Tawzer Dog LLC. www.TawzerDog.com

Ardrey, Robert. (1966). *The Territorial Imperative.* Dell Publishing Co. Inc.; NY.

Barteau, Yvonne. (2007). *Ride the Right Horse: understanding the core equine personalities & how to work with them.* Storey Publishing; North Adam, MA.

Bee, Vanessa. (2013). *3-Minute Horsemanship: 60 amazingly achievable lessons to improve your horse when time is short.* Trafalgar Square Books; North Pomfret, VT.

Bee, Vanessa. (2015) *Over, Under Through: Obstacle Training for Horses: Step-by-Step Exercises for Every Rider.* Trafalgar Square Books; North Pomfret, VT.

Bruce, Georgia. www.clickertraining.org

Budiansky, Stephen. (1997). *The Nature of the Horse: Their Evolution, Intelligence and Behavior.* Phoenix; London.

Burns, Stephanie. (2002). *Move Closer Stay Longer.* Parelli Natural Horsemanship; Pagosa Springs, Colorado. (Excellent if you feel nervous around horses.)

Camp, Joe (2011). *Training with Treats: with relationship & basic training locked in, treats can become an excellent way to enhance good communication.* 14 Hands Press; USA.

Dorrance, Bill and Desmond, Leslie. (2001). *True Horsemanship Through Feel.* First Lyons Press; Guilford, CT.

Hanson, Mark. (2011). *Revealing Your Hidden Horse: a revolutionary approach to understanding your horse.* (Amazon On-Demand Publishing; www.amazon.com.)

Jackson, Jaime. (2002). *Horse Owner's Guide to Natural Hoof Care.* Star Ridge Publishing; Harrison, AR.

King, Callie Rae. (2016). http://www.crktrainingblog.com/

Kurland, Alexandra. www.theclickercenter.com

Levinson, Franklin.
https://www.facebook.com/franklin.levinson

MacLeay, Jennifer. (2003). *Smart Horse: understanding the science of natural horsemanship.* Blood Horse Publications; Lexington, KY.

Mejdell, Cecilie M., Turid Buvik, Grete H.M. Jørgensen, Knut E. Bøe. *Horses can learn to use symbols to communicate their preferences*; http://www.appliedanimalbehaviour.com/article/S0168-1591(16)30219-2/fulltext; (Accessed 28 Sept 2016.)

Miller, Dr Robert M. (1999). *Understanding the Ancient Secrets of the Horse's Mind.* The Russell Meerdink Co. Ltd.; Neenah, WI. (Also look up Dr Miller to find his resources on Foal Imprinting if you'd like to know more about that.)

Newport, Cal. (2011). http://calnewport.com/blog/2011/07/10/the-procrastinating-caveman-what-human-evolution-teaches-us-about-why-we-put-off-work-and-how-to-stop/ (Accessed July 18, 2016)

Parelli, Pat and Linda Parelli. www.parelli.com

Pryor, Karen. (1999). *Don't Shoot the Dog: the new art of teaching and training.* Bantam; New York. (About much more than dogs.)

Pryor, Karen. (2009). *Reaching the Animal Mind: Clicker Training and what it teaches us about all animals.* Scribner; New York.

Pryor, Karen. (2014). *On My Mind: reflections on animal behavior and learning.* Sunshine Books Inc.; Waltham, MA.

Resnick, Carolyn. (2005). *Naked Liberty: Memoirs of my Childhood: the language of movement, communication, and leadership through the way of horses.* Amigo Publications; Los Olivos, CA.

Schneider, Susan M. (2012). *The Science of Consequences: how they affect genes, change the brain and impact our world.* Prometheus Books; New York.

Printed in Great Britain
by Amazon